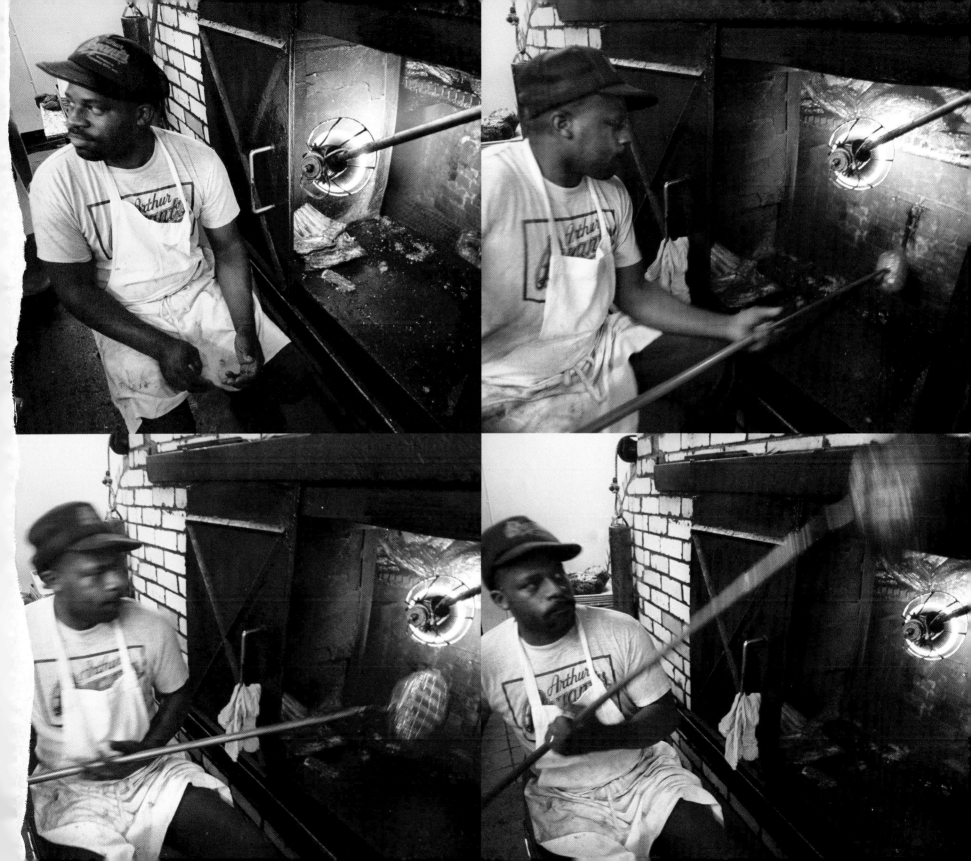

THE

★★★★★★★★★★★ THE ★★★★★★★★★★★

GRAND BARBECUE

A Celebration of the History, Places, Personalities and Techniques of Kansas City Barbecue

BY DOUG WORGUL

THE GRAND BARBECUE
A CELEBRATION OF KANSAS CITY BARBECUE

Written and edited by Doug Worgul
Design and production supervision by Jeff Dodge
Production by River City Studio

Published by KANSAS CITY STAR BOOKS
1729 Grand Boulevard
Kansas City, Missouri, USA 64108

First edition

Library of Congress Control Number: 2001116831

ISBN: 0-9709131-2-5

Printed in the United States of America
By Walsworth Publishing Co.

To order copies, call StarInfo, (816) 234-4636

For more information about this and other fine
books from Kansas City Star Books, visit our Web
site at www.kcstar.com

4R

★ ★ ★ ★ ★ ★ ★ ★ ★ ★ ★

ACKNOWLEDGMENTS

This book is a celebration of Kansas City barbecue. Its only ambition is to extol the virtues of barbecue and some of the people and places, past and present, that have helped make Kansas City the Barbecue Capital of the World. Though there is a fair amount of history in it, it is not really a history text. Though there are some recipes in it, it is not really a cookbook.

Another thing it is not is comprehensive. Half my job in creating this book was writing. That was the fun part. I got to meet a lot of great people and eat a lot of great barbecue. The other half of my job was editing. That part wasn't as fun, because it meant making some hard choices about what to include in the book and what to exclude. Being the newspaper of record for Kansas City for over a century, *The Kansas City Star* has reported and written quite a bit about barbecue. Many of *The Star's* best barbecue stories appear in this book. But not all of them. We just didn't have the space in the book to include them all. So I had to choose some and leave others out.

The same is true of the nearly 100 barbecue joints in the Kansas City area and the hundreds of competitors from the region who actively participate in local and national barbecue contests. Unfortunately, I could not include all their stories in the pages of this book, worthy though all may be. Of necessity, I had to be selective.

Among the many people without whose reporting, hard work and dedication I could not have completed this book are the following: Jim Barcus, Donald Bradley, Beverly Bundy, Brian Burnes, Lauren Chapin, Ardie Davis, Derek Donovan, Tim Engle, Tim Finn, Jim Fussell, Joe Henderson, Tim Janicke, Paul Kirk, Steve Kraske, Victoria Sizemore Long, Brian McTavish, Jennifer Mann, John Martellaro, Gentry Mullen, Steve Paul, Kathleen Purvis, Mary Schmitt, Jill Wendholt Silva, Joyce Smith, Judy Thomas, Karen Uhlenhuth, Carolyn Wells, Gary Wells, and Susan White.

Unless otherwise noted, all the contributed articles in this book are by current reporters and editors of *The Kansas City Star*.

Special thanks to Ed "Fast Eddy" Maurin (www.fasteddysbbq.com) for his lead on the "Smoky" Joe Armato story, and to Dan Turner for his lead on the "Poppa" Miller story.

I'm sincerely grateful for Laura Christensen and her research assistance, for Mike Humphrey and his speedy reporting and for Tim Engle and his thorough copyediting and friendship.

Finally, I'd like to thank Doug Weaver, who called my bluff; Jeff Dodge, for his tasty book design; the girls, for the joy they have given me; and Rebecca, for her patience and faith.

—Doug Worgul
Kansas City, April 2001

★ ★ ★ ★ ★ ★ ★ ★ ★ ★

TABLE OF CONTENTS

INTRODUCTION

FOR ALL THAT MAY COME

Barbecue is the food of celebration.

From ancient times on, barbecue has been the food of choice when there's something worth making a big deal about. *"The men have returned from the hunt with a buffalo. Let's barbecue!"* *"The president is coming to town! Let's barbecue!"*

Barbecue takes the toughest, meanest cuts of meat — not aristocratic cuts with names like *porterhouse*, but common cuts like the *butt* — and makes them not just edible but delectable. This alchemy is achieved with the smoke of hardwood and the sweat of hard work. And by the time it's done, the feasting and drinking that follow are well-earned. It is, in and of itself, a feat worth celebrating.

Smack in the middle of the front page of the very first edition of *The Kansas City Evening Star*, September 18, 1880, is an article with the headline "The Grand Barbecue." It seems those early Kansas Citians were so elated at the opening of a railroad connection — a project that took eight years to complete — that "a grand old fashioned barbecue was determined upon... the event celebrated in a manner and style peculiarly characteristic of Kansas City pluck and enterprise."

It's been a part of our identity from the beginning. And now barbecue is one of the few things left in Kansas City that's truly ours.

We used to be a cowtown, but the cows are gone now. Jazz was ours once, back when you could dance to it, but it skipped town when rock-n-roll showed up. Many of our hometown companies have been bought out by faceless foreign interests. Even the Country Club Plaza and Brookside shops are owned by out-of-towners who are probably still looking for the corner of 12th Street and Vine.

Much of what has traditionally defined Kansas City has faded or been traded away. Swallowed up in the swells of an increasingly homogenized, corporatized and globalized culture.

But global conforming has not yet swept away all things uniquely Kansas City. Barbecue stems the tide. National barbecue chains have found this market to be tougher than an undercooked brisket. A few years back we laughed some guy named Tony Roma out of town when he claimed his restaurant had the best ribs in the world.

Then there's the McRib, which, no matter how they advertise it, will never be confused with barbecue. The phrase "fast food" cannot, in fact, be used when talking about barbecue. It is the slowest of all foods. That's one of the reasons barbecue resists the forces of McDonaldization.

Barbecue is an expression of some of life's most enduring values, values mostly incompatible with the business strategies of global corporations: tradition, hospitality, patience, craftsmanship, creativity and community.

Barbecue is such hard work, so inefficient and so very slow that it makes no sense to go to all that trouble unless you intend to feed lots of people. Thus it is inherently communal. Once you've gathered all those people together, well, then you wait and wait and wait some more, because barbecue is rarely done on time. And while you're waiting you talk with one another. You get to know one another better. You become more of a community.

And when the barbecue is ready to eat, it's time to celebrate.

Near the end of that story about "the grand barbecue" celebration in the first edition of *The Star* is a sentence that is practically biblical in its prose and promise. Reading it, you might think it's describing heaven. It is, in fact, describing Kansas City. It concludes with these words: *"where a sumptuous feast of fat things is prepared for all that may come."*

Clockwise from top left: Barbecue on a bike on its way to the 2000 American Royal Barbecue Contest; Fine tuning the fire at the Raytown State Championship Barbecue Cookoff; Members of Grace United Methodist Church in Lee's Summit do a little two-step at a church barbecue; Tasting ribs before judging at the Blue Springs Blaze Off.

CHAPTER ONE

MADE IN AMERICA

ORIGINS

In his book *The American Language* (1919), H.L. Mencken states that the word *barbecue* came from the Spanish word *barbacoa*, which he theorized had its roots in the word *boucan*, from the language of the Taino people, who are native to islands in the Caribbean.

Mencken appears to have been on the right track. However, barbecue scholar C. Clark "Smoky" Hale believes there is a more direct Taino ancestor of our modern word *barbecue* than the word *boucan*. In a fine article on the origins of barbecue (found on-line at www.barbecuen.com) Hale goes right to the source: Peter Guanikeyu Torres, president and council chief of the Taino Indigenous Nation of the Caribbean and Florida. Torres breaks down the Taino word *barabicu* this way: b*a* from *baba* (father); *ra* from *Yara* (fire); *bi* from *bibi* (beginning) and *cu* from *guacu* (the sacred fire). Thus the phrase "Taino barabicu" means the "sacred fire pit."

It is no surprise to me that the etymology of the word *barbecue* would reveal that it is sacred in its origin. Anybody who has sunk his teeth into a beef sandwich at Lil' Jake's already knows this. It is indeed a religious experience.

★ ★ ★ ★ ★

In researching his awesome book *Southern Food* (1993) John Egerton found that early in the 1600s English colonists in Virginia made a law prohibiting the discharge of firearms at a barbecue. Which is a really good law, because when you're trying to concentrate on a slab of ribs, you don't want to be distracted by the possibility that you might get shot.

Writing in the year 1728 about the boundary between Virginia and North Carolina, William Byrd noted in his *History of the Dividing Line* that "The only business here is raising of hogs, which is managed with the least of trouble and affords the diet they are most fond of. The truth of it is, the inhabitants of North Carolina devour so much of the swine's flesh that it fills them full of gross humors."

I'll spare you an historical analysis of the phrase "gross humors."

Pork became a favorite in the colonial South because pigs were easy to care for and provided lots of meat for relatively little effort. The only thing was, you pretty much had to cook the entire pig at once because there was no way to keep meat fresh until such time as you needed it. The technique of heavily spicing, then slowly smoking whole hogs not only resulted in a very tasty meal, it greatly reduced the likelihood that contaminants would spoil the meat.

By 1735, when Alexander Pope wrote *Second Satire of the Second Book of Homer*, American barbecue was well established, well known and well liked. In the best line of the book, Pope practically shouts "Send me, Gods! A whole pig barbecued!"

I've heard customers at Gates respond with this same phrase just after the lady behind the counter yells, "Hi! May I help you?"

BARBECUE

REVOLUTION

It's hard to imagine George Washington having any fun. In none of the portraits painted during his lifetime is the man smiling. He appears always to be shouldering the weight of a nation's hopes and fears. But a reading of Washington's personal diaries reveals a real man, a whole person, a fellow who liked to have a good time as much as the next guy.

The Father of Our Country notes in his journal that on May 27, 1769, he traveled to Alexandria, Virginia, to attend a "barbicue." It must have been quite the affair because he stayed all night. In fact, while Ol' George was enjoying his "barbicue" he was cleaning up in a card game. He notes in his diary that he won a game of "eights."

In May of 1774, Washington went with some friends to another barbecue. And here we begin to see a pattern emerge. Each time the future first president attended a barbecue, his journal indicates that for a day or two afterward he laid low and didn't do anything worth noting. Nothing. Then, according to the journal, he went to church. It appears that he needed a day or so to recover from his hearty partying — and then, perhaps, he felt the need for repentance.

There's a phrase often used to describe George Washington; "First in war. First in peace. First in the hearts of his countrymen." Seems he was also first in line at the barbecue table. Perhaps when, as a lad, he chopped down his father's cherry tree he was just hoping to use the wood to smoke a brisket.

Barbecue events were firmly established as a part of American social life by the mid-18th century. In their book *A History of the City of Brooklyn and King's County* (1894), Stephen Ostrander and Alexander Black described one such event.

Again on June 4, 1766, being the anniversary of the King's birthday, a celebration was had by the patriots on the commons where the City Hall now stands. A barbecue was held, whereat a roast ox, beer, and punch were provided in sufficient quantities to supply the wants of all. The greatest enthusiasm prevailed.

Another early mention of barbecue in American history appears in the journal of a young Englishman traveling in the Colonies in 1774:

About noon a Pilot Boat came along side in invite the Captn. to a Barbecue. I went with him and have been highly diverted. These Barbecues are Hogs, roasted whole. This was under a large Tree. A great number of young people met together with a Fiddle and Banjo played by two Negroes, with plenty of Toddy, which both Men and Women seemed to be very fond of. I believe they have danced and drunk till there are few sober amongst them. I am sorry I was not able to join them.

AN AMERICAN
TRADITION

The American tradition of celebrating important civic and family events with a barbecue is as old as the Republic itself. Accounts of America's early victories and the biographies of some of our nation's early heroes include descriptions of some of these celebrations.

In A General History of Duchess County from 1609 to 1876, written in 1877 by Philip Henry Smith, we find this rather amusing story, the first part of which is immediately and painfully familiar to all husbands who have hosted their in-laws for a cook-out and undercooked or burned the brisket:

"At the close of the Revolution a 'barbecue' was held at Dover Plains. A man named Grant gave the ox, which was spitted and roasted whole. Speeches were delivered and a great concourse of people came together. Although the cooking was none of the best and the flesh was either raw or burned to a crisp, the patriotism of the people led them to pronounce it excellent.

When a herald passed through the country announcing the surrender of Burgoyne, the tidings met with a hearty response from every patriot. Bonfires, illuminations, and the thunder of artillery everywhere demonstrated the joy that was felt throughout the land. The people of Pawling Precinct instituted a barbecue in commemoration of the event. A hole was dug in the bank near the site of the residence of Richard Chapman, Esq., a fire was built therein, and a fine, full-grown bullock was spitted before it. The cooking was not a pronounced success, but Pawling charged upon it with all her chivalry. Patriotic speeches were made, patriotic songs sung, and patriotic toasts drank in profusion; and nothing prevented the thundering of cannon, but the want of cannon and powder. The Tories growled with rage, but kept at a respectful distance.

Thus the day wore off. The remnant of the carcass was given to some fellows from the West Mountain, who, by dint of exertion, managed to get it about half a mile; wearied with their efforts, and unctuous with grease and perspiration, they laid it down to discuss the matter. They finally concluded to leave it until the next morning. During the night a pack of hungry dogs undertook the task of demolishing the carcass and struck a balance before morning."

★ ★ ★ ★ ★ ★ ★ ★ ★ ★

In 1808 Thomas Jefferson's granddaughter, Ellen Randolph, wrote him to tell him of a "great barbecue" that was to be held in Charlottesville on the Fourth of July that year. By 1820, Independence Day barbecues had become elaborate events that included readings of the Declaration of Independence, balloon launches and dancing.

When Abraham Lincoln's parents, Thomas Lincoln and Nancy Hanks, were married on June 12, 1806, they celebrated their vows with a barbecue. Christopher Graham, a guest at the wedding, later remembered it this way:

"We had bear meat, venison, wild turkey and ducks, eggs wild and tame, maple sugar lumps tied on a string to bite off for coffee or whisky, syrup in big gourds, peach and honey, a sheep barbecued whole over coals of wood burned in a pit, and covered with green boughs to keep the juices in; and a race for the whisky bottle."

— From Lincoln: *The Prairie Years* (1927)
by Carl Sandburg

★ ★ ★ ★ ★ ★ ★ ★ ★ ★

A VIRGINIA

BARBECUE

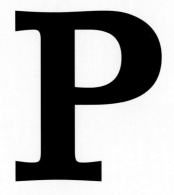erhaps the best contemporary description of an early nineteenth century barbecue is in Charles Lanman's 1856 book *Adventures in the Wilds of the United States and British American Provinces*, in the chapter titled "A Virginia Barbecue."

It's important to remember when reading this passage that slavery was still very much a part of life in the United States when this was written. In spite of the glowing language and pastoral imagery used in this description, the picture we're left with is, in the end, ugly, because the event was possible only through the forced labor of black slaves.

That said, it is interesting to note that all the elements we have come to associate with barbecue are present here, 150 years ago; meat slowly cooking over wood coals, the gathering of family and friends, laughter, music, and libation.

The word barbecue is said to be derived from a combination of two French words, signifying from the head to the tail, or rather, "according to the modern," the whole figure, or the whole hog.

By some, this species of entertainment is thought to have originated in the West India Islands. However this may be, it is quite certain that it was first introduced into this country by the early settlers of Virginia; and though well known throughout all the Southern States, it is commonly looked upon as a "pleasant invention" of the Old Dominion.

The idea was evidently conceived by a rural popu-lation, and in a district where villages and the ordinary public buildings of the present time were few and far between. For purposes of business or pleasure, the people found it necessary, or advisable, to meet togeth-er in masses, at stated periods; and as these meetings were made a kind of rural festival, and as the animals served up on such occasions were commonly roasted entire, it was not unnatural that the feast should even-tually have become known as a barbecue.

Of the genus barbecue, as it exists at the present time, we believe there are only two varieties known to the people of Virginia, and these may be denominated as social and political. The social barbecue is some-times given at the expense of a single individual, but more commonly by a party of gentlemen, who desire to gratify their friends and neighbors by a social enter-tainment. At times, the ceremony of issuing written invitations is attended to; but, generally speaking, it is understood that all the yeomanry of the immediate neighborhood, with their wives and children, will be heartily welcomed, and a spirit of perfect equality invariably prevails. The spot ordinarily selected for the meeting is an oaken grove in some pleasant vale, and the first movement is to dispatch to the selected place a crowd of faithful Negroes, for the purpose of making all the necessary arrangements. If the barbecue is given at the expense of half a dozen gentlemen, you may safely calculate that at least thirty servants will be employed in bringing together the good things.

Those belonging to one of the entertainers will probably make their appearance on the ground with a wagon load of fine young pigs: others will bring two or three lambs, others some fine old whisky and a supply of wine, others the necessary table-cloths, plates, knives and forks, others an abundance of bread, and others will make their appearance in the capacity of musicians. When the necessaries are thus collected, the servants all join hands and proceed with their important duties.

They first dig a pit, four feet wide, two or three deep, and as long as they require, into which they throw a quantity of wood, for the purpose of obtaining therefrom a bed of burning coals. This done, the more expert kitchen Negroes proceed to roast (by laying

laughing girls under their charge; and children of every age, from the wild and boisterous boy to little girls just old enough to totter after a butterfly. One, or perhaps two hours, are then spent by the multitude in playing rural games, in social converse, in telling stories, or in discussing the news of the day. Finally, the pigs and lambs have all been roasted, and the feast is ready; whereupon there followeth as busy and satisfactory a scene as can well be imagined.

After it is ended, the Negroes come into rightful possession of all the tables and the abundance of good things left over; and, having quietly invited a number of their friends, with their families, they proceed to enjoy their portion of the entertainment, which is generally concluded by a regular Negro frolic, with banjo and fiddle, in a neighboring grove. In due time, after the more substantial feature of the barbecue has been enjoyed, the musicians are summoned to their allotted places, and the entire party of ladies and gentlemen proceed to trip the light fantastic toe. The exercise con-

only in the following particulars: It is generally gotten up by the leaders of one of the political parties, and speeches take the place of dancing, although ladies in considerable numbers are in attendance. Previous to the appointed day for the political barbecue, a placard is nailed to all the barn doors and blacksmith shops in the district or county where it occurs, to the effect that "several distinguished speakers will be present on the occasion," and that the people of all parties are invited to be present. If the entertainers on this occasion are of the Whig party, the first speech is delivered by a Whig orator, and it is no uncommon sight to see this gentleman standing literally on the stamp. After he has taken his seat, he is usually followed by a brother orator of the Democratic party; and so, alternately, are the principles of the prevailing parties fully discussed. Generally, the greatest decorum exists, not only among the speakers but among the listeners; and if severe remarks are dropped in the heat of debate, they are not commonly considered of sufficient consequence to

The social barbecue is sometimes given at the expense of a single individual,
but more commonly by a party of gentlemen, who desire to gratify their friends and neighbors by a social entertainment.

them upon sticks across the fires) the various animals prepared for the occasion. In the meantime, all the other arrangements are progressing, such as spreading the white cloths upon the temporary board tables, and clearing a place for dancing.

The guests begin to assemble about ten o'clock, and by noon there is hardly a tree within hailing distance of the centre of attraction, to which a horse is not fastened. The assembly is quite large; and white dresses and scarlet shawls are as numerous as the summer flowers upon the neighboring hills. Old men are here with their wives and daughters, in whose veins floweth the best of aristocratic blood; young husbands with their wives; unmarried gentlemen with a bevy of

tinues for hours, and white-haired men and little girls are seen wending their way through the intricate mazes of the country dance and the Virginia reel. As the sun nears the horizon, the more advanced members of the party quietly take their departure, leaving a cloud of dust behind them on the road. By the time the last day-flower has closed its petal, the young men and maidens have entire possession of the barbecue ground; and having wound up the last reel by the light of the newly-risen moon, they dismiss the musicians, gather together their hats and shawls, and. with many a song and jest return to their several homes.

With regard to the political barbecue, we have to remark that it differs from the one already described

create a breach between personal friends. There are times, however, when even the political barbecue is concluded by a dance; but as the crowd is then particularly miscellaneous, the hilarity which usually prevails is apt to be a little too boisterous. When given in the autumn, new cider usually takes the place of more stimulating drinks (so far as the multitude are concerned, at any rate,) and when this is the case, it is very seldom that any improprieties occur. But a genuine Virginia barbecue, whether of a political or social character, is a rural entertainment which deserves far more praise than censure, and we know of none which affords the stranger a better opportunity of studying the character of the yeomanry of the Southern States.

POLITICS

AS USUAL

The political barbecue appears to have been perfected in 1840 by the presidential campaign of William Henry Harrison. Harrison's advance men would travel throughout the country staging enormous barbecues to coincide with their candidate's speeches. Apparently, once they had selected a site, they would erect a temporary log cabin, which Harrison had adopted as the symbol of his campaign. Then folks from the town and country-side would be invited to a huge feast of barbecue and drinking.

The largest of these events was held in Wheeling, West Virginia, where 30,000 potential voters were wooed. Accounts of the occasion tell of 360 hams, 20 calves, 25 sheep, 1,500 pounds of beef, 8,000 pounds of bread and 4,500 pies being served.

But not everyone loved these big bashes. The Rev. J. D. Long, an anti-slavery minister of the time, complained about them in a newspaper editorial: "There is not much difficulty in the South in raising money for a barbecue, or to buy whiskey for political purposes; but when funds are wanted for a library, that is quite another question."

In spite of the good reverend's protestations, barbecues were becoming ever more popular as civic and political events, and as the population moved West, barbecues began to occur with increasing frequency in the country's western states and territories.

One of the early accounts of a barbecue in Missouri describes an event in Jefferson City on August 10, 1847, at which one Maj. William Gilpin speechified at some length about U.S. relations with Mexico. Clearly this was a clever strategy on the part of the cooks to greatly increase the crowd's restlessness and eagerness to eat.

News stories of a barbecue held to celebrate the arrival of the railroad in Kansas Territory (probably the Hannibal & St. Joseph Railroad, which reached Kansas on February 14, 1859) fail to mention who the guest speakers were, but the food appears to have left a lasting impression: "Six beeves, twenty hogs, and over fifty sheep, pigs and lambs were roasted. There were also prepared more than 100 boiled hams, several thousand loaves of bread, cakes by the hundred, besides sundry other delicacies to tickle the palate and help make the occasion one long to be remembered by all those present."

Apparently french fries didn't arrive in Kansas Territory until later.

★ ★ ★ ★ ★ ★ ★ ★ ★ ★

SCENES FROM A

KANSAS
CHILDHOOD

William F. "Buffalo Bill" Cody was one of America's first self-invented Wild West heroes and one of Kansas' earliest white residents. His 1879 autobiography, *The Life and Adventures of Buffalo Bill,* includes the following account of Kansas barbecues during his childhood:

In anticipation of the early passage of what was known as the "Enabling Act of Kansas Territory," which was then pending before Congress, my father, in the fall of 1853, took his family from the farm of his brother and settled them at the post in Kansas, where he at once set about erecting suitable log buildings. In the succeeding winter the act was passed which opened up the territory for settlement, and father immediately pre-empted the claim on which he was living.

During the summer of this year we lived in our little log house, and father continued to trade with the Indians, who became very friendly; hardly a day passed without a social visit from them. I spent a great deal of time with the Indian boys, who taught me how to shoot with the bow and arrow, at which I became quite expert. I also took part in all their sports, and learned to talk the Kickapoo language to some extent.

Father desired to express his friendship for these Indians, and accordingly arranged a grand barbecue for them. He invited them all to be present on a certain day, which they were; he then presented them with two fat beeves, to be killed and cooked in the various Indian styles. Mother made several large boilers full of coffee, which she gave to them, together with sugar and bread. There were about two hundred Indians in attendance at the feast, and they all enjoyed and appreciated it. In the evening they had one of their grand fantastic war dances, which greatly amused me, it being the first sight of the kind I had ever witnessed.

My Uncle Elijah and quite a large number of gentlemen and ladies came over from Weston to attend the entertainment. The Indians returned to their homes well satisfied.

July 3, 1869, is one of the most important dates in Kansas City history. On that day the Hannibal Bridge was opened. It was the first permanent bridge across the Missouri River. The economic and cultural impact of the bridge is difficult to overstate. It transformed a small frontier outpost into a boom town almost overnight. One part of Kansas City culture, however, was well-established by that time. Kansas Citians celebrated their significant civic events with *barbecue*. Sixty years after the event, Bernard Donnelly of *The Kansas City Star* described the day with these words:

Then the celebrators reformed and marched to the barbecue grounds, located in Col. Steen's pasture at the eastern terminus of Ottawa Street - near what is now Twelfth Street and Troost Avenue. The procession had been joined by twelve floats representing different phases of the bridge's construction. Then there were speeches. The speaker's stand, by the way, was directly south of the bar table. After some music, Judge William Douglass introduced Gen. John A. McClearnand of Illinois, the orator of the day, who spoke prophetically of the future of Kansas City and the West. Carl Schurz, then senator from Missouri, was called upon to speak, but declaring that he had come to see and hear rather than to talk, he turned Gen. Grant's phrase "Let us have peace" into "Let us have dinner," and it being noon everyone consented and "attacked the tables."

The Kansas City Times was one of the city's leading newspapers in the late 19th century. On October 11, 1876, the following notice appeared encouraging the citizenry to attend a rather large civic barbecue.

"Fifteen beeves, one hundred and twenty sheep, twenty five hogs, and five car loads of turkeys and chickens have been provided for tomorrow's barbecue on the Exposition grounds. Everybody invited."

A read through the *Times* from that era reveals some entertaining glimpses into Kansas City life at a time when cows and cowboys roamed the streets.

"Kansas City is entitled to cheap meat and good meat. This city is the great meat market of the world and there is no reason for charging a higher price here than is paid in New York, Boston or Philadelphia."

November 4, 1877

"The city has been overrun with cow boys during the past few days."

August 20, 1878

"Crazy Alice was released from the county jail yesterday, and is now skipping around the railroad yards in West Kansas once more."

August 22, 1878

"Has Kansas City a crack base ball nine? 'Nein.'"

September 28, 1878

I don't know about you, but I'm just dying to know more about Crazy Alice.

—D.W.

CHAPTER TWO

HOW KANSAS CITY BECAME THE
BARBECUE CAPITAL
OF THE WORLD

Barbecue became an integral and intimate part of Kansas City's identity as the fortuitous result of a variety of geographical, political, economic and social forces and circumstances.

The only part of the United States with a significant barbecue tradition is the South and regions heavily influenced by the South. While Missouri is not now generally considered a Southern state, it was a slave state, and its early identity was primarily formed by the politics and collective cultural memory of Southerners who migrated to this area during the early-to-mid-19th century.

The confluence of rivers and railroads in Kansas City was another major determinant in our becoming a barbecue capital. In the 19th century, buyers and sellers used the rivers and railroads to transport livestock in and out of Kansas City, and a thriving meatpacking industry developed. The ready availability of cheap meat, and the abundance of hardwood trees with which this area had also been blessed, provided barbecuers with the two fundamental necessities of their craft.

But it was the migration of African-Americans to the region, between 1879 and 1881, and then again in the early decades of the 20th century, that was the single most important factor in barbecue becoming such a distinct part of Kansas City culture.

Because barbecue was, at the time, a method of preparing meat that was practiced almost exclusively by slaves, when former slaves and descendants of slaves moved to this part of the country their barbecue skills became the basis of significant economic activity. Barbecue was a product that they alone could provide.

This entrepreneurial activity was facilitated first by Kansas City's determinedly optimistic frontier culture and encouraged again later by the anything-goes policies of the Pendergast political machine.

It seems, however, that for decades the proliferation of barbecue joints was taken for granted by Kansas Citians themselves. Especially white Kansas Citians. It wasn't until word of our barbecue excellence began to spread to other parts of the country that we ourselves began to appreciate it.

Left: Old Municipal Stadium.
Right page, from left: Stockyards in the 1870s; employees of a turn of the century packing house; downtown Kansas City 1906.

During the 1950s and '60s, the old Municipal Stadium, at 22nd and Brooklyn, was close enough to some of the area's many barbecue stands that announcers broadcasting ballgames over the radio could smell the sweet smoke. They'd mention this to their listeners, and people throughout the Midwest began to get the idea that if you were hungry for barbecue, Kansas City was a good place to be.

Likewise, sportswriters visiting to cover baseball games with their hometown teams Kansas City they sought out Bryant's, or other joints, to experience authentic Kansas City barbecue for themselves.

Not long after that, a creative, culinarily inclined Kansas City psychologist named Rich Davis began foolin' around with recipes for a barbecue sauce. When he finally hit on a formula he liked, he put it in bottles and started selling it around town. Then he started selling it in other towns. And soon K.C. Masterpiece was being sold in supermarkets nationwide. comes to town to broadcast a Chiefs game he inevitably mentions the aroma of barbecue floating in from the parking lot, reminding the world once more of our preeminence in all things barbecue.

Finally, in the 1980s the Kansas City Barbeque Society (KCBS) was founded which has become the premier sanctioning body in the increasingly popular sport of barbecue competition. At the same time Kansas City became host to two of the top contests in the

would also smell the smoke and sometimes seek out its source. Their findings would frequently end up in their newspaper stories, thus informing readers in the far corners of the country that barbecue was one of the things that made Kansas City unique.

Then, in 1974, Calvin Trillin, a sublimely gifted writer and Kansas City native, penned an article for *The New Yorker* magazine that sealed our fate and put us on the map. The essay, "American Fried," extolled the virtues of Kansas City barbecue in general and Arthur Bryant's barbecue in particular. And it did so in language that was witty and hip. Thereafter, when affluent, well-educated, well-traveled readers of *The New Yorker* happened to visit The association of barbecue with Kansas City was further solidified.

Surprisingly enough, the building of Arrowhead Stadium in the 1970s played a role in spreading our barbecue fame. Without the acres and acres of parking space surrounding the stadium, the tailgating tradition that has become a ritual prior to each Kansas City Chiefs home game would not have been possible. Not surprisingly, barbecue — honest-to-goodness barbecue, smokers and all — has become as much a part of Kansas City-style tailgating as hamburgers and hotdogs are elsewhere.

And, as in the old days at Municipal Stadium, when John Madden or Al Michaels sport: the American Royal Barbecue and the Great Lenexa Barbeque Battle. These contests and the KCBS have significantly enhanced Kansas City's barbecue image across the nation.

These are the anthropological and sociological facts of how Kansas City became the barbecue capital of the world. But facts and truth are not one and the same. Ultimately, answering the question of how and why barbecue came to belong to Kansas City is like answering a child when she asks her mother, "Why am I your daughter?"

The best and most accurate answer is "Because God wanted it that way."

HENRY PERRY

THE BARBECUE KING

Kansas City might not even be Kansas City if not for Henry Perry.

Clearly, somebody had to be the first to open a barbecue joint in town. But what if that somebody hadn't been Henry Perry? Maybe that somebody wouldn't have known just when to turn the briskets and the butts, or maybe they would have taken them out of the pit too soon. Maybe that somebody would have used too much vinegar in the sauce or too little cayenne. Or maybe they wouldn't have stuck with it when things got tough. And barbecue might never have had the chance to catch on here. Then, disgusted with this barbecue blight, Kansas Citians might just have packed up and taken their tastebuds elsewhere.

If somebody other than Henry Perry had been the first to open a barbecue joint in Kansas City, God might just have gotten exasperated and decided, "Look, if you can't get it right, I'll let some other city be The Barbecue Capital of The World."

Thank God it was Henry Perry.

Henry Perry was born in 1875 in Shelby County, Tennessee. Memphis is the main city in Shelby County. And the main fact of life is the Mississippi River.

By the time he was 15 years old Henry Perry had landed a job as a cook on one of the steamboats that traveled the river. The boat docked in cities up and down the Mississippi, giving young Henry the opportunity to see places and people that other boys his age could only dream of, and by the time he was 16, he had lost interest in going back to Shelby County. He just kept on following the river, ending up in Chicago and then Minneapolis.

It took Henry Perry another 16 years of drifting to find his destiny here in Kansas City.

He was an experienced and hard-working kitchen hand, and soon after arriving in 1907 he found a job as a porter in a Quality Hill saloon. But a restlessness still flowed in him, and he knew he wouldn't be happy busing dishes very long.

So it wasn't very long after that that Henry Perry was selling barbecue from a stand on Banks Street alley.

In Shelby County, Tennessee, barbecue was probably as much a part of life as the river itself, so maybe that's where the idea came from. Or maybe he learned the art of preparing and smoking meat from some old pitmaster in some sleepy little town somewhere along the Mississippi.

But it's just as likely that Henry Perry didn't get the notion of making a living by selling barbecue until he got to Kansas City. Barbecue was already here. It was a part of civic celebrations, church events and family reunions. It was ingrained in the cultural consciousness of hundreds of Kansas Citians who, like Henry Perry himself, had come to this place from the American South.

Maybe Henry Perry was ready to settle down. And when he saw that Kansas Citians had an appetite for barbecue he got the idea that someone could make some pretty good money at it if they sold a good product at a good price. It just might be the thing that would let him get comfortable for awhile.

Call it Divine Providence.

In the fullness of time, the lives of Henry Perry and Kansas City came together and were changed.

The Banks alley barbecue stand was successful enough that Perry soon needed more room to operate. He moved his enterprise to a place at 17th and Lydia.

Arthur Bryant, who years later learned barbecue from Henry Perry, once said that Perry "started out with a hole in the ground." This description suggests that early on Perry did his cooking outdoors. Old-timers remember Perry wrapping his barbecue in newspapers. And Perry's advertisements from this period promise customers barbecued "possom," woodchuck, and raccoon. It was, by today's standards, a rather crude affair.

But it all worked somehow.

Soon Perry had competitors; other black men from the South who knew how to barbecue and were eager to imitate Perry's success.

In February 1932, 25 years after Henry Perry first opened his barbecue business, *The Call*, Kansas City's leading black newspaper, published an interview with Perry. The article notes that there were in Kansas City at that time "more than a thousand barbecue stands."

Clearly Henry Perry had started something.

But though there may have been pretenders to the throne, Perry was "The Barbecue King." And in *The Call* Perry explained why.

One reason, he said, "is the special way I prepare my meats. Cooking only over a fire made from hickory and oak woods the meat gets that delicious flavor which is the cause of the tremendous popularity of barbecued meats."

Apparently the popularity of Perry's product had come to the attention of commercial manufacturing houses that had begun selling special barbecue ovens "with plenty of attractive doodads." ▶

Barbecue King —

HENRY PERRY

In an 1932 interview with *The Call*, Henry Perry claimed that the barbecue stand he opened in Kansas City in 1907 was the first commercial barbecue joint in the United States. He said, "As far as I know, at the time there was not another such establishment anywhere. I believe that I was the first to enter the field."

Alas, it seems unlikely that Mr. Perry's was America's first barbecue joint.

Folks in Ayden, North Carolina, say that in 1830 Skilton Dennis opened the very first commercial barbecue business. A 1984 article in *National Geographic* attempts to validate this claim, but its description of Mr. Dennis' operation makes it sound as if it were more of a catering enterprise than a restaurant, or even a stand.

A strong case may be made that Harry Green was America's first barbecue restaurateur. According to *Kentucky Monthly* magazine, Green opened a place in Owensboro, Kentucky, in 1890.

All of this is, to a certain extent, speculation. We'll never know for sure who opened America's first barbecue joint. We can safely assume, however, that whoever it was, he was black.

At the turn of the century, the only people who really knew anything at all about barbecue were African-American men. That's because for hundreds of years making barbecue considered too menial for whites and too difficult for women was a task performed exclusively by male slaves of African origin. (See our discussion of barbecue and race on Page 60.)

Left: Henry Perry's joint at 19th and Highland. This photograph was taken in 1940 as part of a Works Progress Administration project documenting real estate in major American cities. The man holding the identification number is a WPA employee.

★ ★ ★ ★ ★ ★ ★ ★ ★ ★

The Call pointed out that "Mr. Perry has been offered such ovens by competitors who wished to trade the new-fangled devices for a course in the Perry style of barbecuing."

Perry's response reflected the confidence that comes with years of experience: "I told them that I wouldn't even have one of the things in my place. There is only one way to cook barbecue and that is the way I am doing it, over a wood fire, with properly constructed oven and pit."

In the 1920s Henry Perry moved his operation to 19th and Highland. According to Arthur Bryant, he worked out of an old streetcar for awhile then moved into a building. He became an increasingly important part of the African-American business community and earned a reputation for generosity, in part by hosting a barbecue picnic for neighborhood children every Fourth of July.

He also acquired a reputation for being a tough, no-nonsense kind of guy. He posted a sign in his restaurant that announced: "My business is to serve you, not to entertain you."

One story has him working the counter at the restaurant when some poor fellow pulled a gun on him in a misguided attempt to rob the place. Perry is said to have produced his own gun from beneath the counter, whereupon he shot the man dead.

Perry might have considered dousing the thief with some of his barbecue sauce. Apparently it was so peppery it "brought tears to people's eyes."

In 1931 Henry Perry suffered a stroke that left him partially paralyzed on one side. This was not the first of his health problems. Years earlier he had lived for a time in Bonner Springs, Kansas, hoping that the country air would help him with chronic ailments. He attributed his "miraculous" recovery from his stroke to a homemade remedy suggested to him by a man, perhaps a customer, who had had too much to drink. Perry decided to try the cure in spite of the fellow's intoxicated state because he had become frustrated that other treatments had failed.

Henry Perry's barbecue kingdom eventually included three restaurants. And among the members of his court were Charlie and Arthur Bryant and Arthur Pinkard. The Bryants eventually started their own joint; Pinkard went on to work for George Gates, founder of the Gates barbecue empire.

Near the end of his life Henry Perry commented on his career in the barbecue business. "I made lots of money," he said. "And I made lots of friends ranging from humble neighbors to members of the monied groups."

Henry Perry died on March 22, 1940. He was 66 years old. He was buried on the banks of the Mississippi in Osceola, Arkansas, just across the river from Shelby County.

In its 1932 feature, *The Call* observed that the popularity of Henry Perry's barbecue crossed traditional social dividing lines. Kansas City, it seems, was united in this regard.

"With a trade about equally divided between white and black, Mr. Perry serves both high and low. Swanky limousines, gleaming with nickel and glossy back, rub shoulders at the curb outside the Perry stand with pre-historic Model-T Fords. Liveried chauffeurs gaze haughtily at humble self-drivers but all have the common ambition to sink their teeth in a bit of Perry's succulent barbecue."

"POPPA" MILLER

KING HENRY II

or over 50 years the story that Henry Perry was the first to open a commercial barbecue establishment in Kansas City has been accepted as fact. But an intriguing bit of history, discovered in 1996 by Dan Turner, an instructor in Johnson County Community College's culinary arts program, poses something of a challenge to Perry's claim.

The story is told by Bob Miller, a retired soldier and civil servant who lives in Leavenworth, Kansas. The story is about his father, Henry Miller.

Henry Miller was born in Oklahoma in 1861. He arrived in Kansas City in 1890, 17 years *before* Henry Perry. An account of Henry Miller's life, written by Bob Miller, indicates that his father was selling barbecue from his house in Kansas City around the turn of the century. Was this a commercial establishment? Probably not. Was it a commercial endeavor? Certainly.

Henry Miller was probably not Kansas City's first barbecue restaurateur. But a case can be made that he was Kansas City's first barbecue entrepreneur. Here is Bob Miller's story, exactly as he wrote it, describing his father's contribution to Kansas City's barbecue heritage:

THE HISTORY OF POPPA MILLER

AND THE OLD FASHIONED SOUTHERN STYLE BARBECUE
As told and remembered by my father, Henry Miller,
the Barbecue King

Known the world over, it is with great pleasure that I, Bob Miller, share the history of the man who is my father and my ideal person.

Who is Henry Miller? Henry Miller was one of three sons (having Ed and Clarence as brothers). His mother, [Maria] an African born woman and former slave. His father a full-blooded Cherokee Indian named Cushenberry.

They met in the Carolinas and traveled through Louisiana, Arkansas and Oklahoma. A great amount of his life was spent in Fort Smith, Little Rock and Oklahoma. He also told me about some short stays in Hot Springs, Ark. His family sold barbecue on the street and in restaurants of Fort Smith, Little Rock and Oklahoma.

After leaving Fort Smith, he wandered and worked 10 years in Oklahoma, then an Indian territory. Henry Miller was fluent in several Indian languages and was fluent in French and German. Traveling North [after] the 10 year period, Henry entered Kansas City on a train. He cooked at several Kansas City hotels and restaurants. He also sold barbecue behind the house where he lived in Kansas City, Mo. He was also a master stone mason and had built many barbecue pits throughout the Kansas City area.

He cooked for several years in Kansas City restaurants and hotels. A few of these were the old Savoy in 1903, the Coates House on Broadway and the old Wishbone Restaurant.

My father told me he was the cook that made the original Wishbone salad dressing. He would make the dressing often in his restaurant. He left Kansas City and traveled to Denver and Colorado Springs. He worked at the Savoy in Denver and later at the Broadmore in Colorado Springs. He made several trips between Kansas City and Denver. Finally, Henry Miller moved to Leavenworth and got married to my mother [Clifton] and raised three sons.

He worked as Chief Cook in the officers' mess at Townsend Hall at Fort Leavenworth, Ks. He also worked at several hotels as a chef. He owned a barbecue restaurant in Leavenworth. He got a job cooking for Fred Harvey at Harvey House in Leavenworth, then returned to Denver and cooked for about a year back at the Shirley Savoy restaurant. He then went back to Leavenworth.

He opened another barbecue behind his home at 302 Dakota Street. This was a log cabin. At this time, World War II was right around the corner.

He bought a gas station at 4th and Pawnee Street, and built onto the existing structure a barbecue pit and was

Left: Poppa Miller in the 1940s.

in business. Serving the world's best barbecue. World War II started and Fort Leavenworth was growing like crazy. Army barracks were everywhere at the Reception Center. People came from all over the world to Leavenworth. The Barbecue King was only two blocks away, and how they ate! Business was booming 24 hours a day.

When I wasn't at school I was at the restaurant working and learning everything I could about cooking. We served thousands each week. He spent a lot of time cooking at state capitals and governors state dinners. He was hired very often to cook and being away added work for my mother and the other hired help.

Barbecue restaurants popped up everywhere. Ribs, briskets and chickens were served as this is what the people wanted to eat.

In the 1940s there were a lot of people throughout the state of Kansas and other states contracting food poisons. There was not one reported or documented case of food poisoning from my father's restaurant. The state of Kansas wanted to know why there was not any reported case of food poisoning from my father's restaurant. My father was summoned to the Kansas state capital to answer questions, why people were getting sick. His answer was that because of the shortage of imported spices, people bought "c" ration cans of catsup by the cases. Soldier cooks sold them. They were using catsup, tomato puree and their tomato product in barbecue sauces. There was no refrigeration being used in those sauces. That is where KC barbecue came in. Jazz and barbecue, World War II and making the fast dollar bill is what happened to old fashioned Southern style barbecue. The old barbecue masters died off and did not tell anyone their secrets. My father made me make the barbecue sauce the last two years of his life. I only tried a short cut one time and my father caught me. It was a bad time for me. He gave me the recipe a year before he gave it to my mother after 20 years of marriage.

Henry Miller was a close friend of Charlie Bryant. He and Charlie would have their weekly get-togethers and sometimes Mr. Gates of 19th and Vine would join them. The word got out, if you wanted to know anything about barbecue, all you need to do is call Henry Miller in Leavenworth, Ks. Those that really knew him knew that his theory was "the more, the better." There is still a pit at the Savoy that he built.

Now we all know how catsup, puree paste got into barbecue sauces. Today sauces aren't even cooked. Most sauces are mixed loaded with preservatives and put into about three styles of glass and shipped. I call these sauces Johnny-Come-Lately sauces. They come from everywhere. I was very lucky to have received Poppa Miller's famous recipe when I was only 16 years old.

Poppa Miller's sauce never had to take short-cuts in creating the master formula since 1872.

Ever since tomato catsup was introduced into today's modern barbecue sauce, people have been misled about barbecue sauce. Catsup is thick and lays on top of the meat or food it's used on. Real old-fashioned barbecue sauce has no tomatoes in its contents. It is much thinner and is put on the meats with a brush. The sauce penetrates into the meat for real barbecue taste. You don't get the two different items mixed up. Real barbecue is where "finger-lickin' good" originated.

★ ★ ★ ★ ★

Henry Miller was indeed a remarkable man. He was 70 years old when his son, Bob, was born. He was 6 feet 7 inches tall and weighed 340 pounds. When boxer Jack Johnson was serving time in the prison at Fort Leavenworth, Henry Miller learned boxing from him.

Bob says that his father lived on what is now Benton Boulevard when he first sold barbecue in Kansas City. Poppa's opposition to tomato-based sauces never wavered. When asked to divulge the secrets of his father's sauce recipe, Bob says it starts with vinegar and then you add "a few other things" and that's all he'll say. Dan Turner swears by the stuff. He says there's nothing better on barbecue brisket.

Bob doesn't know if Henry Miller knew Henry Perry, but he was, Bob recalls, friends with Arthur Pinkard. "Mr. Pinkard would stay at our house here in Leavenworth," Bob says. "They got along real good. They played cards when he was here."

The Arthur Pinkard connection is particularly interesting. Pinkard learned barbecue from Henry Perry. And George Gates, patriarch of the Gates barbecue empire, learned barbecue from Arthur Pinkard. As a tribute to his contribution to the Gates family's fortunes, Pinkard's picture hangs in the entryway of each of Gates restaurant.

Ollie Gates doesn't specifically remember his father, George, getting together regularly with Charlie Bryant and Henry Miller, as mentioned in Bob Miller's account. "My dad didn't care too much for Charlie Bryant," Gates recalls. "But Dad knew lots of people, and he might have met with them [Miller and Bryant] from time to time."

Poppa Miller died in 1951 at age 90. Bob says that his father remained amazingly strong and active right up until the end. "Even when he was 90 we would still go out together with our two-man saw to cut hickory, oak and apple wood for the barbecue," Bob says. "He was cooking barbecue on the day he died."

★ ★ ★ ★ ★ ★ ★ ★ ★

ARTHUR PINKARD

MYSTERY MAN

Soon there will be no one left who remembers anything at all about Arthur Pinkard. He died a half century ago. And if you ask people what they remember about the man, well, it seems that even when he was alive no one knew much about him.

"He was a loner," says Arzelia Gates, matriarch of the Gates barbecue dynasty. "He kept to himself and he never married or had children."

Mrs. Gates is 92 years old at this writing. Fifty-five years ago, in 1946, she and her husband George bought a run-down barbecue joint called Ol' Kentuck Bar-B-Q from a guy named Johnny Thomas. Arthur Pinkard came with the place.

"He was old *then*," recalls Ollie Gates, who was 14 when his folks got into the barbecue business. "He had to be in his late 60s. But he taught my father and me what barbecue is all about. And that's why we have his picture hanging in all our restaurants."

That's him in the big black and white photograph, standing at the barbecue pit in his white cook's uniform, looking a bit surprised and perhaps a little annoyed that someone is interrupting his work with a camera.

Many of the histories written about Kansas City barbecue include the apocryphal story of how George Gates learned the barbecue biz from Henry Perry.

That story is false.

"As far as I know, my father and Henry Perry never even met," says Ollie Gates. "But Arthur Pinkard *did* learn from Henry Perry. He was a student of Henry Perry's. And that is how we came to learn how to barbecue the Henry Perry way."

According to Gates, the Henry Perry method of barbecuing means slow-cooking the meat directly over wood coals. "This means that the meat juices drip onto the coals," Gates explains. "As far as I know Bryant's and Gates are the only places in town that use this method."

In the early 1950s, Arthur Pinkard retired and left town. By then the Gates family had fixed up the restaurant quite nicely and was well on its way. Mrs. Gates says that they soon lost touch with their former pitmaster. And it wasn't long before they got word that he'd died.

"It's kind of sad, really," reflects Ollie Gates. "He never got to see what he helped get started."

★ ★ ★ ★ ★ ★ ★ ★ ★ ★

JOE AND WILLY

THE ORIGINAL SMOKY JOE

About the time Henrys Perry and Miller were establishing their respective barbecue domains, a scrawny Italian kid named Joe showed up in Kansas City, alone, his dreams his only companions.

Joseph Armato was born in Sambuca, Sicily, on June 21, 1895. By the time he was 15 the Mediterranean island was no longer big enough for him. The boy was restless and stubbornly independent, and he longed for a better life.

He'd heard of America. He'd heard that if you worked hard you could make a life for yourself there. And if there was one thing Joe Armato knew about it was hard work. He made up his mind. He was going to America. And if his family wanted to stay behind in Sicily, well, then he was going anyway.

Who knows why he chose Kansas City? Perhaps he'd heard stories about the Wild West and this was as far west as he could get. Maybe, because he didn't speak English, he somehow got on the wrong train and ended up here. But around 1910, Joe Armato arrived. No family. No money. And no reason he could think of that his dreams wouldn't come true.

He landed a job on the railroad. The work was backbreaking, dirty and sometimes dangerous, but Joe stayed with it. He saved every penny, and by the time he was 17 he was able to buy a horse and a cart. He quit the railroad and started his own business selling ice and coal from the cart.

Pete Armato is Joe's son. Pete is 75. He owns an engraving shop on Independence Avenue and despite his age he shows up for work every day and shows no signs of slowing down. That work ethic came from his father, Pete says. "When we was growin' up, all we heard was, 'You got to own your own business.' That was his big thing. He wanted us to be independent."

Pete says that after a few years selling coal and ice, his father had saved enough money to buy a restaurant. He opened a place at 607 E. Fifth Street and started selling barbecue. Soon Joe's joint had become a local favorite.

That's where Willy comes in.

Pete Armato doesn't know much about Willy. Not even his last name. The stories Joe told his children about that time in his life didn't include that information. But Joe made it clear that Willy was one of the main reasons people came to his restaurant.

The place was particularly popular with the policemen who patrolled the neighborhood. According to Pete, around lunchtime a cop might poke his head in the door and shout "Got any ribs, Joe?"

"Yeah, I got some ribs," Joe would shout back.

"Who made 'em?"

"Willy made 'em."

"Then we'll have some."

And the cop would come on inside, followed by several others.

Willy's barbecue was served on slices of Italian bread cut diagonally and mopped with Joe's special sauce.

"I remember that sauce," Pete says. "It was kinda like a combination of a Gates and a Bryant's. Not too sweet, with some spice to it.

"He charged 20 cents for a sandwich and 15 cents for a bowl of chili. I remember him tellin' us that."

Apparently, Willy wasn't the only cook in the joint. During the 10 years he owned the place, Joe honed his own cooking skills and earned a reputation for fixing fine food. The folks at the old Riverside racetrack invited him up to sell his fare to fans on race days.

One time the actor Buddy Rogers stopped in for meal. "My father said that he marveled at the food and said he would tell all his Hollywood pals about it," Pete recalls.

Pete's wife, Theresa, says that her father-in-law perfected and passed down to her a recipe for Italian sausage that remains a closely guarded family secret to this day. "It's the best," she says confidently. "And I'm the only one who knows how to make it."

"He probably wasn't the first to open a barbecue joint in town," Pete says about his father. "But he certainly was *one* of the first. They called him 'Smoky Joe' because he was known for his barbecue and he always smelled like smoke. I do know for sure he was the very first 'Smoky Joe.'

"Coming to Kansas City from Sicily was a good thing for my father. He made a good life for himself here. He never went back."

Left: Joe Armato waiting on a customer in his Fifth Street barbecue joint. Willy stands guard at the barbecue pit in the corner. The photograph was probably taken in 1915. Above: a beat cop patrols Fifthe Street, circa 1915.

Ernest Hemingway never wrote about Kansas City barbecue. He never wrote much about Kansas City in general, despite his seven-month apprenticeship in 1917-18 as a cub reporter at *The Kansas City Star*.

Hemingway did once recount how he had spent much of his winter here deliberately making his way through the seven-page menu of a Chinese restaurant. That gastronomic adventure provided his introduction to sea slugs and proper chow mein.

At long last, we can report that documentary evidence proves that Kansas City barbecue was once on Hemingway's mind. It comes on a scrap of paper that is part of the manuscript collection of the Hemingway Archives at the John F. Kennedy Library in Boston.

Very simply, in Hemingway's own handwriting, is the scrawl "BBQ." (We're not making this up.) Along with that is a hard-to-read address on Troost Avenue (possibly 3402), a couple of Kansas City phone numbers and a notation that reads something like "7 sandw. for 1.00." (On the same piece of paper there are also a few handwritten sentences about suicide and the idea of philosophy in books — he was against it - but those relatively more substantial digressions are hardly worth going into here.)

The scrap probably dates from either 1928 or 1931, when Hemingway spent weeks at a time in Kansas City awaiting the births of his second and third sons. During the earlier of those stays he was working on the last sections of his great novel, *A Farewell to Arms*. During the second, he toiled on his book about Spain and bullfighting, *Death in the Afternoon*.

Can it be that one of those American classics was fueled by a sauce-drenched feed of ribs and fries? That Hemingway and barbecue might have had a "damned fine time together"? To paraphrase one of the most famous last lines in literature, it's certainly pretty to think so.

— Steve Paul

ARTHUR BRYANT'S

'THE BEST DAMN RESTAURANT IN THE WORLD'

Arthur Bryant's is the most famous barbecue joint on the face of the earth. Like it or not and it seems that folks either *love* Bryant's or *hate* Bryant's Bryant's is the standard by which Kansas Citians judge all other barbecue establishments.

Listen to people describe a new barbecue joint sometime:

"Well, the food was pretty good. Not as good as Bryant's, but you know, it was all right. The place looked alot better than Bryant's, but it was kind of corporate. Kind of suburban."

Bryant's is the standard because it is what many, if not most, people think a barbecue joint should be: plain and simple to the point of being austere, straightforward and unpretentious, with a focus on food, not on niceties. And even though it is no longer owned by its African-American founding family, and is now the property of a white-owned restaurant company, it retains a genuine authenticity that cannot be faked. Or duplicated. It has changed so little over the years that standing in line at Bryant's place at 18th and Brooklyn is like standing in a timeline extending all the way back to Henry Perry's first barbecue establishment.

★ ★ ★ ★ ★

It hasn't always been Arthur Bryant's. For a long time the place was known as Charlie Bryant's, and there's still a generation of Kansas Citians that remembers it that way. Arthur's older brother Charlie got his start in the barbecue business working for Henry Perry himself. When Perry died in 1940 Charlie took over the operation, and when Charlie retired in 1946, Arthur took over.

Arthur Bryant was born in 1902 on an East Texas (Branchville) farm. "Lord that was poor country," he said once in an interview with *The Star.* "The people was poor. The schools was poor. The land wasn't worth much. I had to run away from home to go to college. It was the only way out."

The college he escaped to and graduated from was Prairie View A&M. After graduating in 1931, he was offered a job but decided to do a little traveling first. He came up to see Charlie who was living here in Kansas City, and that was the end of that. Arthur Bryant never went back, and we're the richer for it.

Charlie was working for Henry Perry. Evidently the older Bryant's work habits had impressed Mr. Perry, because he gave Arthur a job, too.

"They were the greatest barbecue men I ever knew. I disagreed some with the sauce they used and some of their methods, but they wouldn't listen. I thought some about what I would do different if I went into the business. But I never would have thought about opening a place while they were around and take away some of their business. It wouldn't have been the right thing."

"Old Man Perry and my brother used to make the sauce way too hot. You could tell by the way the people frowned. It should be a pleasure. I told them that, but they wouldn't believe me."

He fixed the place up a little, too. But only a little.

"That's just not barbecue when you got them plush seats and the dark interior. That wouldn't be no grease house that way. You can put in an air conditioner and plastic-top tables if you want, but you can't get too fancy or you get away from what the place is all about."

★ ★ ★ ★ ★

The story could end here and you'd have learned all that's really important about Bryant's. It's a grease house. Simple as that.

And in most ways the man responsible for it was just as straightforward and no-nonsense.

He came to work early and stayed late. And in between he worked hard. There was no part of the business that he couldn't do and didn't do.

He never married.

"I'm a self-made man," Arthur Bryant once explained. "I make my own pickles, cut my own potatoes. I do everything I can myself. This is a personal business. I have to know what's going

Arthur Bryant in his grease house, 1975.

on. I don't hire me a barbecue man to come in here and do it. *I'm* the barbecue man. The only time I left was when my dad died in Texas. I put my most trusted man in charge, and the first night he burned the place down."

Many nights Bryant slept over at the restaurant on a cot in a back room. He kept a bottle of brandy back there. And it's where he felt most at home.

Besides, leaving late could be dangerous.

"In 1949 I left one night and a man was waiting for me under my car," Bryant recalled. "He came up behind as I was getting in, but I had my own .45 and I told him to lay down his stuff. I sent him up for five years."

★ ★ ★ ★ ★

Over time, Bryant's single-minded dedication to his barbecue created a large and loyal local following.

When he was in town, Count Basie used to order ribs from Bryant's. Legend has it that he'd spit on 'em to prevent his band mates from stealing 'em between sets.

Harry Truman was a regular customer.

And so was a kid named Calvin Trillin.

Lots of white folks think that Calvin Trillin is the reason Arthur Bryant's is so famous. But you could make a strong argument that Arthur Bryant's is the reason Calvin Trillin is so famous.

Trillin grew up in Kansas City during the late '30s and '40s. After graduating from high school in 1953 he left town to attend Yale and to seek his fortune as a journalist.

He was a good reporter, and he soon found himself writing for *The New Yorker*, a magazine known for its literary content and its hip, literate readers. It wasn't long before Trillin had his own large and loyal following.

But Calvin Trillin's career really took off after 1974, when he wrote an essay titled "American Fried," in which he made the now-famous statement that Arthur Bryant's is the "best damn restaurant in the world."

Suddenly Bryant's was trendy. And so was Trillin.

Hollywood heavyweights Robert Redford and Jack Nicholson made a point of stopping at Bryant's when they were in town. Just to show that they were in the know.

World-famous chef Craig Claiborne arranged

to have 300 pounds of Bryant's ribs flown to New York to serve to visiting French chefs.

And in October 1979, President Jimmy Carter arrived unannounced for lunch during a Kansas City visit, apparently leaving town with an extra sandwich handed to him by Arthur Bryant himself.

And when Trillin came back to Kansas City for a visit, he'd stop by, too. On one such occasion he and Bryant slipped into the back room for a glass of cognac.

"He's a fan of mine. And I'm a fan of his," said Bryant.

★ ★ ★ ★ ★

By 1981 Arthur Bryant was getting tired. He'd had heart problems for a long time. But he hadn't yet figured out how to take it easy.

He tried to convert his operation into a take-out-only business, but his customers refused to allow it. Bryant's right-hand man at the time, Richard France, said, "They stayed and ate here standing up, so we brought the chairs back in."

Bryant had been in the habit of shutting the place down every January so that he and his employees could enjoy a little time off, but even

so, the years and the hard work were catching up with him.

His eyesight was failing, and his employees said that he got around the restaurant mostly by memory.

"After you go so long, you get worn out," he told a reporter. "You try to slow down. But it's your life. You can't just go sit down and quit. You'd go crazy. It's what makes me happy. I feel like I've done everything the way I wanted it. There ain't nothing in the world I'd rather be doing."

Arthur Bryant died on December 28, 1982.

He arrived at work at dawn as he had every morning since joining his brother Charlie in the business back in 1931. Around 9 o'clock Richard France went to check on him and found that he'd collapsed. He was rushed to Truman Medical Center, but it was too late. He died of heart attack.

"The boss man is passed," said France. "The legend is gone."

★ ★ ★ ★ ★

In January 1983 Arthur Bryant's beloved grease house was closed as it was every January. But that year it seemed likely that the enterprise Henry Perry had started 76 years earlier would never open again.

Bryant had left the business to his niece, Dorthea Bryant. She'd been helping her uncle at the restaurant for several years, but now she was unsure how to proceed.

Richard France, who had worked for Bryant's since 1955 since he was 16 years old had quit to open his own joint in Independence. For a long time France had practically run the place and his knowledge and experience would be sorely missed.

Ultimately, Dorthea decided to lease the business to a restaurant management company headed by Bill Rauschelbach and Gary Berbiglia (and, at the time, Preston Kerr) in exchange for rent and a percentage of the restaurant's earnings. But the relationship between Dorthea and the management company immediately soured.

A complicated soap opera of manipulation, exploitation, lawsuits, and counter suits ensued, lasting years and threatening to close the venerable joint for good.

It took a while but peace was finally negotiated. Dorthea Bryant eventually sold the business to the Rauschelbach group, while retaining rights to market Bryant's barbecue sauce. She has since retired and now lives in Texas.

Bill Rauschelbach and his partners take seriously the legacy they've acquired. They've made savvy business decisions to enhance the overall profitability of the venture, such as opening a second Bryant's in a popular Kansas City-area casino. There's even been some talk of opening a third site in Johnson County.

Meanwhile the joint at 18th and Brooklyn just keeps on keepin' on. The unsmiling, efficient and slightly impatient employees pile the tender, juicy beef about a mile high on slices of cheap white bread, just as they have for four generations. The bright-orange sauce is as gritty and polarizing as ever. The fries are just as fat and just as fattening. And the floor is still greasy.

Arthur Bryant would probably be OK with things as they are, because they're pretty much the same as they've always been.

Bryant was once asked what it takes to make great barbecue. He seemed annoyed at the question, as if the answer should be obvious.

"Just what you see me doing here," he said.

★ ★ ★ ★ ★ ★ ★ ★ ★ ★

FROM THE WHITE HOUSE

TO THE GREASE HOUSE

On June 14, 1994, President Bill Clinton came to Kansas City to unveil a welfare-reform package.

But to this day the debate lingers over what the most memorable part of his trip was: the speech or what happened afterward.

After leaving the downtown bank where Clinton delivered his address, the presidential motorcade sped northward to Kansas City International Airport and Air Force One. But early on, Clinton's limousine took a sharp detour, unnoticed by the trailing press corps, that left the rest of his motorcade in the dust.

The president's unscheduled destination: Gates Bar-B-Q at 12th Street and Brooklyn Avenue.

While panicked reporters scrambled to uncover the location of the wayward chief executive, the president strode into Gates, where he was greeted with the traditional welcome.

"Hi, may I help you?"

You bet, the obviously desirous president declared. He ordered the mixed-plate special: ribs, ham, beef, bread and fries, and washed it all down with what owner Ollie Gates called "that red soda water."

Chalk up another signal moment in the history of Kansas City barbecue. Everyone knows that presidents routinely dine on such culinary delights as Hudson Valley *foie gras* or Blanquette of Gingered Salmon at the White House or in the world's most exclusive dining establishments.

But let it be said that many Oval Office occupants, not to mention numerous candidates eager to work there, hold a deep-seated and well-documented lust for those irresistible strips of tender pork or beef we simply call "ribs." And let there be no doubt that they love to smother those meaty bones with that magical hickory-flavored potion we call "the sauce."

Harry Truman, from nearby Independence, launched the presidential barbecue parade with numerous stops in area establishments. In 1979, Jimmy Carter ignited a furious Kansas City rib-

joint competition when he stopped by Arthur Bryant's for a beef sandwich and fries.

Not to be outdone, his Democratic presidential rival in 1980, Ted Kennedy, swung by a Gates a short time later. There he removed his tie, rolled up his sleeves and attacked a plate of ribs with trademark Kennedy gusto.

President-to-be George Bush (the elder) was a customer of Bobby Bell's barbecue. He proclaimed to a *Star* reporter in 1985 that he was "one of the great specialists on barbecue."

In 1988, just days before he won the vice presidency, Dan Quayle forked over $188.29 in cash for an order of 10 slabs of ribs, 10 pounds of baked beans and six chickens at a Gates in Independence. Presumably he shared the order with his security entourage.

Clinton takes the all-time trophy. His ravenous love of barbecue caused him to haul untold trays of ribs and fries and beef over the years back to Washington so that he could spread the joy of Kansas City "Q" to unsuspecting East Coasters.

All of which brings us to the current occupant of the Oval Office, George W. Bush. To be sure, Dubya has sterling barbecue bonafides. He met his wife, Laura Welch, at a backyard barbecue in Midland, Texas. Campaign spending records from 2000 reveal that Bush often served barbecue at campaign events.

But in March 2001, during his first visit to Kansas City as president, he committed a noxious culinary *faux pas* when he chose a bland North Kansas City breakfast restaurant, a franchise eatery, no less, as the site of his unscheduled visit for the day.

If it weren't for the president's well-known predilection for barbecue, the critics would have howled.

For the record, Bush may have enjoyed barbecue from elsewhere around the nation. But until he tastes the real stuff in Kansas City, he ain't tasted nothin'.

— Steve Kraske

CALVIN
TRILLIN

ENDS

O ther than the folks with grease on their shoes and smoke in their clothes who've been up all night makin' the stuff, Calvin Trillin is more responsible for Kansas City's reputation as a barbecue capital than anyone.

This is his hometown. He grew up between 70th Terrace and Gregory, graduated from Southwest High School in 1953 and then went on to Yale for college, to please his father, in spite of wanting to go to Mizzou "like everyone else."

But by the time he'd left Kansas City to find fortune and fame as a journalist, Trillin had acquired a taste for Kresge's chili dogs, Winstead's hamburgers and Bryant's barbecue. And it was writing about Kresge's chili dogs, Winstead's hamburgers and Bryant's barbecue, among other things, that resulted in his finding fortune and fame as a journalist.

In a 1974 essay for *The New Yorker*, Trillin made the statement that Arthur Bryant's is "the best damn restaurant in the world."

Critics have since speculated that he must have been kidding. That he couldn't have been serious. That surely he was joking.

These are the anxieties of the insecure. Trillin admits that sometimes his writing about food has been taken too seriously. After all, he concedes, "I'm not what my wife, Alice, calls a grown-up food writer."

But back in the 1970s and '80s, back when Kansas City was feeling even more, well, insecure about itself, Trillin confessed to loving the idea that his praise of Bryant's and Winstead's might undermine the efforts of some poor Chamber of Commerce staffer to promote Kansas City's more "sophisticated" restaurants.

And though he's lived in New York for decades, Kansas City is where he's from and who he is.

Recently he's become interested in the decision to remove the big plastic Hereford from its pedestal overlooking the West Bottoms, a decision that seems to symbolize Kansas City's embarrassment about its "cowtown" image. But Trillin has never been embarrassed about Kansas City.

Maybe we ought to put a statue of him on the pedestal where the bull used to be, just to remind us that this is a pretty fine place, capable, in fact, of producing one of the best damn writers in the world.

Kansas City's very own distinctive barbecue tradition. Arthur Bryant's invented 'em. Gates won't serve 'em. Purists eschew them. The rest of us chew them.

The Gospel According to Trillin says that customers at Bryant's used to be able to help themselves to burnt ends from a pile next to the meat slicer, where they'd been trimmed off the briskets. They were free. And they were delicious. Chewy. Smoky. Dark and mysterious.

Over the years they gained such a loyal following that customers began to demand burnt ends at other joints in town. And savvy barbecue entrepreneurs were quick to oblige.

Except for Gates.

"We try not to burn our meat" is Gates' official party line.

Believe it or not, there's actually been some debate as to whether burnt ends are legitimate barbecue. Well, I'll put my pork butt on the line and say "Of course they are!"

Burnt ends are as much barbecue as the briskets or pork shoulders they are cut from. In fact, given how intensely they taste of wood smoke, you could say (and I do) they are the very concentrated essence of barbecue.

Sadly, however, what many barbecue places call burnt ends are really just chopped-up pieces of regular barbecue beef and/or pork, mixed with sauce.

But those aren't *burnt* ends. Those are chopped-up pieces of regular barbecue beef and/or pork, mixed with sauce. They're more like Sloppy Joes. In fact, a few joints call 'em Smoky Joes.

Real burnt ends are, well, *burnt*. And it's the fact that they're burnt that gives them their rich smoky flavor and wonderful crunchy chewiness.

Choosy barbecue lovers choose chewy. They'll go for *real* burnt ends every time.

— D.W.

OLLIE GATES

THE BUILDER

When Ollie Gates, Kansas City's most successful barbecue entrepreneur, talks about his achievements and his dreams, you realize that barbecue is beside the point.

Ollie Gates is a builder. The joy in his career has come not so much from perfecting the smoking and saucing of briskets and ribs as much as from building the pits in which the briskets and ribs are smoked, building a factory to produce the sauce, building new systems to improve the way a restaurant works, and building a thriving business that has given jobs and careers to hundreds of people.

Arzelia Gates, Ollie's 91-year-old mother, says that building things has been her son's passion since he was a toddler.

"Oh, yes," she recalls. "He'd build a tower with his blocks and just study it. Then he'd knock it down and build a better one."

"Build a Better One" has been an enduring theme in Ollie Gates' life.

One of the first things he wanted to build better was the house he grew up in. It was the house his great-grandfather built, a source of family pride.

"I suppose it was something to be proud of," Gates says. "But when I was a kid all I knew was

that the house was way too small and it had no indoor toilet. I dreamed of building walls from the house to the toilet outside."

When he was old enough to work a trowel, he helped his father plaster houses in neighborhoods north of the river. And later, when he was 14 or 15, he got an after-school and weekend job with a construction contractor putting up dry wall.

"That was a good job for a young kid to have," says Gates. "Building things gave me a sense of accomplishment and purpose."

That's not all. It gave him the chance to drive.

"I found out, after the fact, that Ollie's boss was letting him drive the truck," laughs Mrs. Gates. "That was something he failed to tell me, of course. Because he didn't have his driver's license yet."

Ollie Gates was tall and strong, and all that construction work made him stronger. And because he was a good student and a gifted athlete, after graduating from Kansas City's Lincoln High School in 1949, he was awarded a football scholarship to a college in Maryland.

Who knows how different his life might have turned out if he'd stayed and finished college there in Maryland? Might he have been good enough to play pro football? Might he have stayed on the East Coast, perhaps becoming an engineer or an architect?

God only knows.

It's safe to say that Kansas City would be a far different and far poorer place if Ollie Gates hadn't come back to the Midwest midway through his college career to help his father build a better business. ▶

Ollie Gates is a master bricklayer. In this 1985 photo he is renovating an old building.

But he did come back, because the other thing Ollie Gates is, in addition to being a builder, is a family man.

He transferred to Lincoln University in Jefferson City in 1952 so he could commute back and forth to Kansas City on weekends, allowing him to help his parents grow their barbecue business. Back at school he worked part time as a bricklayer.

"I didn't really want to have anything to do with the barbecue business back then," Ollie Gates admits. "But my folks needed the help. Back then I felt it was an ugly business. It wasn't like it is now."

Of course, Ollie Gates is one of the main reasons barbecue is no longer an ugly business.

★ ★ ★ ★ ★

Arzelia June Smith was born in Rosedale. Her father, Ollie Smith, worked in some of Kansas City's finest hotels, including the Muehlebach. Her mother, Edna Smith, was a matriarch of the St. John AME congregation.

Arzelia attended grade school with George Gates, and in 1926 she married him.

As a young man, George liked to barbecue in the backyard. But, as Mrs. Gates observes, "The entire male population of the United States thinks it can barbecue," so, at the time, she didn't think much of it. It was just a typical husband's hobby — an entertaining way to spend a Sunday afternoon and feed the kids.

As Mrs. Gates tells it, George's backyard barbecues sometimes involved some friendly competition between Mr. Gates and his next-door neighbor.

"They were always bragging at one another boasting that 'My ribs are better than yours' or 'My sauce beats your sauce,' " recalls Mrs. Gates. "One time our neighbor said, 'My barbecue is so good I could open a restaurant.' Well, my husband replied, 'My barbecue is so good I will open a restaurant.' And he did. And that's how it all started."

"That's a great story, isn't it?" smiles Ollie Gates. "There's some truth to it. But it's just a little more complicated than that."

George Gates had worked for years as a waiter on the Rock Island railroad line, says Ollie Gates.

"He worked his way up as far as they would let him go. Back then they didn't let African-Americans hold the title of steward, even though that's the job he was doing. So he was pretty frustrated, and eventually he decided he'd had enough."

George Gates tried different jobs after quitting the railroad, eventually landing a position at the post office. According to Ollie, his father was the first African-American postal clerk in Kansas City. One day, however, one of the supervisors remarked to George, "You've got a white man's job." Gates replied, "Then give it to him," and he quit.

That's when he bought the restaurant, Ollie says.

It was 1946 and the restaurant was named Ol' Kentuck Bar-B-Q. It was at 19th and Vine.

"My dad's original idea was to get into the liquor business," Ollie says. "Ol' Kentuck was just a step away from being a speakeasy. They were selling a lot of bootleg whiskey there. But my mother, being

the moral person she is, decided the whiskey would have to go."

Gates recalls that his father had a business partner when he bought the restaurant, but the relationship lasted only three months.

"That's when my mother got involved," Ollie says. "She was the exchequer and the keeper of the books."

"I did a little of everything," Mrs. Gates remembers. "I didn't ever cook. But I did everything else. I cleaned. I ran the cash register. I waited on the customers. Did everything. It was hard work, but I didn't mind. I was young, and I knew that working for yourself is easier than working for somebody else. I had worked for somebody else since I was 11 years old. It was a chance to do what I thought best, not what somebody else told me."

Ollie says his mother's role was significantly more than that of helpmate to her husband.

"She provided a direction," he says. "My dad was all action but no direction. She had a strong moral center. She was raised properly, and the truth is, my father was barely raised up at all. She had values my dad didn't have."

The barbecue business gave both Arzelia Gates and her husband the opportunity to employ the values of hard work and charity.

"One time a man came into the restaurant looking all sad," Mrs. Gates recalls. "And my husband went up to him and asked him what was wrong. The man said that he was here from Oklahoma to work and that he'd just got a call that his mother had died back home. He said he didn't have the money to buy clothes for the funeral. So my husband went into the back room and changed into a cook's uniform and gave the man the suit he'd been wearing, plus fare to get to Oklahoma."

When reminded of this story Ollie Gates nods his head. He says that such generosity was typical of his parents.

One of Ollie's daughters, who is also his mother's namesake, says that this family tradition of giving is one reason Gates Bar-B-Q has been so involved in civic affairs. "My grandmother set the example," Arzelia Gates says.

The younger Arzelia, 47, is chief marketing officer for the business. She says there's more than one way a company can promote its product. "Of course, you can advertise. And we do that. But another way is to become involved in the community. To give back something to the community that supports you."

This philosophy is the motivation for Ollie Gates' high-profile civic involvement.

Gates served as president of the Kansas City Board of Parks and Recreation from 1979 to 1997, as chairman of the Bruce R. Watkins Foundation board of directors, and as a member of the Missouri Highway and Transportation Commission.

★ ★ ★ ★ ★

Four of Ollie Gates' five children are active in the company. Even Gates grandchildren are getting a head start in the business, including the younger Arzelia's nine year-old daughter, Aspen, who's been given a desk in her mom's office at the company's corporate headquarters. "It's never too early to teach children the value of hard work and to show them that it can be fun and rewarding," says Arzelia.

When asked which of his children or grand-

Far left: George and Arzelia Gates and their daughter Gwendolyn in front of Ol' Kentuck Bar-B-Que. Left: Arzelia Gates working the counter in the late '40s.

1946	George Gates buys Ol' Kentuck Bar-B-Q at 19th and Vine
1949	Moves to 23rd and Charlotte
1951	Back to 19th and Vine to open a tavern
1951	Fire closes the 19th and Vine location; restaurant moves to 24th and Brooklyn until 1957
1954	Second restaurant opens at 12th and Highland
1958	First "from the ground up" restaurant opens at 12th and Brooklyn and name is changed to "Gates and Son Bar-B-Q" to reflect Ollie's increasing involvement
1960	George Gates dies
1962	OG's barbecue restaurant/nightclub opens at 31st and Indiana
1970	OG's closes; new restaurant at 1411 Swope Parkway opens
1971	Acquired office and warehouse space, 4707 Paseo
1972	New restaurant at 103rd and State Line opens
1975	New restaurant at 10th and State Ave. In Kansas City, Kan., opens
1975	Gates Bar-B-Q sauce is introduced in area grocery stores
1975	"College of Barbecue Knowledge" (Rib Tech) is developed to orient and train Gates employees
1979	New restaurant at 10440 E. 40 Highway in Independence
1980	Ollie purchases 12th and Brooklyn site from his mother and sister and builds shopping center there
1986	New restaurant at 216 N. Rawhide in Olathe opens
1991	Las Vegas restaurant opens
1994	Las Vegas restaurant closes
1995	Restaurant at Linwood and Main opens
1997	Olathe restaurant closes
1997	March 4 - Swope Parkway restaurant (plus administrative offices and Rib Tech) closes after the property is condemned by the city for use in the Brush Creek Redevelopment
1999	Ollie appears on Martha Stewart Living TV show
2000	New flagship restaurant at 1325 E. Emanuel Cleaver opens, complete with 20 ft. "Struttin' Man" sign.

★ ★ ★ ★ ★ ★ ★ ★ ★

After graduating from college with a degree in building construction, Gates joined the army and enrolled in its engineering school.

"When I got out of the service and came back here to help my folks, it seemed clear to me that the business could use a dose of engineering," Gates recalls. "For example, they were still making sauce with 'a little of this and a little of that.' Well, the customer could never be sure that the sauce he tasted one time would be the same the next time. We needed consistency."

George Gates at first resisted his son's attempts at standardization, but soon relented. And with Ollie's assistance and leadership, the business began to grow. Over time additional locations were opened and the name of the business was changed from Gates Bar-B-Q to Gates and Son Bar-B-Q to reflect Ollie's role.

One of Ollie's most significant contributions to his family's business has, in fact, helped change the image of the entire barbecue restaurant industry.

Before Ollie Gates came along, barbecue joints were, as he describes them, "dirty, greasy and ugly." He set out to change that.

By insisting on stringent standards of cleanliness and maintenance, by engineering the kitchens and barbecue pits to minimize the circulation and accumulation of smoke and grease, and by modeling the company's new restaurants after, well, other restaurants, as opposed to other barbecue joints, Gates changed the public's perception of barbecue. Gates understood that he was competing with fast-food establishments such as McDonald's and Kentucky Fried Chicken, and that only by emulating their operations could he hope to succeed.

"Frankly, I needed to make a real business out of it," Gates says. "I had five children to send to college. Arthur Bryant could afford to stay where he was. He just had a couple of dogs."

★ ★ ★ ★ ★

Before George Gates died in 1960, he saw the beginning of the company's remarkable growth, which continues to the present.

In 2000 Gates and Son Bar-B-Q christened a new flagship store on Emanuel Cleaver II Parkway. The restaurant is a tribute to the original Ol' Kentuck Bar-B-Q and to African-American business and cultural leaders in Kansas City's past.

After showing the place off for some guests, Ollie Gates stops to clean up some dishes and straighten chairs at one of tables.

"This is a pretty nice place, isn't it?" he says. "But I've already got some ideas for the next place."

children will succeed him when, or if, he retires, Ollie Gates hesitates. "Maybe none of them," he says. "And I wouldn't necessarily blame them if they didn't. This business will take all you've got to give it and more. It's not an easy life. Not if you're doin' it right."

The Gates family sets high standards for itself and for its hundreds of employees. One of Ollie Gates' most significant contributions to his family's business was the introduction of strict business practices and standards.

Above left: Gwendolyn Gates, Ollie Gates, their mother Arzelia Gates, and Ollie Gates' daughter Arzelia Gates at the opening of their new restaurant on Emanuel Cleaver II Parkway.

BARBECUE

Besides barbecue, Kansas City is perhaps best known for jazz. Except that it was never really jazz. It was the blues all along.

Chuck Haddix, host of KCUR-FM's "Fish Fry" ("the best in blues, soul, rhythm & blues, jumpin' jive and zydeco"), says that despite Kansas City's reputation as a jazz town, the blues are the foundation of Kansas City's musical heritage.

"Look at Big Joe Turner," Haddix says. "He was shoutin' the blues. Basie was swingin' the blues. And Jay McShann was jumpin' the blues. It was all the blues. Even Charlie Parker played the blues."

Haddix has heard them all in his job as sound recording specialist at the Marr Sound Archive at the University of Missouri-Kansas City.

"Jay [McShann] has always said that Kansas City is where jazz and blues came together," Haddix points out.

Kansas City is also where music and barbecue come together. According to Haddix both were an integral part of the social fabric of African-American life in Kansas City from the early-20th century on into the 1930s.

"Many of the barbecue joints were also important venues for blues and jazz," says Haddix. "The music flowed from the joints like smoke."

Haddix has researched the subject and says that Ol' Kentuck Bar-B-Q, which later became Gates Bar-B-Q, was one of the joints that featured live music.

Gates has since adopted The Struttin' Man as its corporate logo, a concept based on Louis Armstrong's song "Struttin' With Some Bar-B-Q."

In Armstrong's tune, and in others that followed, a reference to barbecue was frequently a double entendre referring to sex or to a sexually desirable person.

And just as you seldom see anyone unhappy at a barbecue joint or a backyard barbecue or a barbecue contest, it's rare to see anyone blue when they're listening to the blues. Barbecue and music belong together because they both bring people together. If you need proof of this, I suggest you visit B.B.'s Lawnside Barbecue or the Grand Emporium this weekend. Better yet, tonight!

Barbecue is the food of celebration, and the blues are the soundtrack of celebration.

There have been scores of songs — most of them blues songs — written about barbecue. Here are some of my faves:

"Bar-B-Cutie" Evan Johns & the h-Bombs

"Barbecue Any Old Time" Blind Boy Fuller #2 (Brownie McGhee)

"Barbecue Bess" Golden Age Jazz Band

"Barbecue Blues" John Hammond

"Barbecued Ribs" The Riffs

"Bar-B-Q Sauce" Sam Price

"Bar-B-Que Man" Sonny Stitt

"Burnin'" Count Basie Orchestra

"Hickory Wind" br5-49 (This is by far the prettiest song on the list. Actually, it's the only pretty song on the list.)

"Hot Barbecue" Brother Jack McDuff

"Hot Sauce" Son Seals

"I Love Bar-B-Q" The Guy Brothers & Orchestra

"Kansas City" (Inexplicably, barbecue is not mentioned in this classic. I put it on the list anyway, because any song about Kansas City is by extension a song about barbecue. This tune has been recorded over 300 times. My favorite versions are by — in alphabetical order — the Beatles, Dick Dale, the original by Wilbert Harrison, Jan and Dean, Albert King, Jimmy Witherspoon, Muddy Waters and Bob Wills.)

"Riffin' at the Bar-B-Q" King Cole's Swingsters

"Smells Like Bar-B-Q" Big Joe and the Dynaflows

"Smoke Gets in Your Eyes" (This standard has been recorded over 700 times. My favorite version is by the Platters.)

"Smoke House Blues" Jelly Roll Morton

"Smoke House" Benny Goodman

"Somebody To Love You" Delbert McClinton (A great song. Listen to it - you'll know why it's on the list.)

"Stomach Ache" Buddy Guy, with Junior Wells

"Struttin' With Some Bar-B-Q" Louis Armstrong

"Too Much Barbeque" Big Twist and the Mellow Fellows

"Who Stole the Hot Sauce" Chubby Carrier

— D.W.

★ ★ ★ ★ ★ ★ ★ ★ ★ ★

ANTHONY RIEKE

THE SURVIVOR

Rosedale Bar-B-Q is for sale.

That's the rumor. Perhaps by now it's been sold. And as sad as it is that this most venerable of Kansas City barbecue joints might pass from the Rieke family which has owned it since July 4, 1936 the day it first opened it's not really surprising. These things happen. Business conditions change. People get tired. Even ol' Anthony Rieke himself probably wouldn't be too upset about it, if he were still alive. If he was anything, Anthony Rieke was a tough-minded survivor. He understood that you have to make hard choices, that you can't get all emotional about business. But when he opened the place way back then, back in the darkest days of the Depression, well, he could never have guessed that the place — which at first wasn't much more than a hot dog stand — would someday sell for over a million dollars. Maybe two million.

That's the rumor.

In 1932 Anthony Rieke, like thousands of others, was out of work. He was 27 years old and he'd spent a lot of time in the unemployment line with nothing to show for it. Finally, to make ends meet, he went back to doing the only thing he knew, selling vegetables from a truck down at the City Market, just as his parents did.

Driving back and forth in his truck from the vegetable garden to the market, Rieke used to pass this little building on Southwest Boulevard. It was just a plywood shack, really. But it gave him an idea. They were selling root beer out of the place, and Rieke started thinking that if he had a place like that, maybe even that place, well, he could make some improvements and, who knows, maybe he could make a go of it.

He got the owners to rent it to him, and he started selling hot dogs and beer. But when the health department found out that the shanty had no sewage system, they shut him down.

Some months later, Rieke went back to the owners to try to rent the place again, but it had already been leased. Which was good luck for Kansas City because it forced Rieke to consider other options.

The solution to Rieke's dilemma was the vacant lot right next door to his former hot dog stand. He leased the lot for $20 a month and on it he built his own little place where he and his brother-in-law, Anthony Sieleman, established the enterprise that eventually became Rosedale Bar-B-Q.

At first they called the joint The Bucket Shop. If you brought your own bucket they'd fill it up with beer for 25 cents.

About a half-mile down the road from The Bucket Shop a guy named "Fatty" Sharp had his own shop where he sold smoked meats for a living. And every night as he was driving home, Anthony Rieke would catch a good whiff of that meat smokin,' and that got him to thinking again.

"It seemed like a good idea, so I had a little barbecue oven put in," Rieke said years later. "But then I said to my brother-in-law 'I don't know nothing about barbecue. Who's gonna do the cookin'?' He said, 'You are.' So I bought me a few ribs and I learned how." ▶

Folks have been lining up for Rosedale ribs ever since.

Turns out Anthony Rieke not only had a knack for making great barbecue, he had a knack for making great barbecue makers. Some of Kansas City's best barbecue restaurateurs got their start working at Rosedale Bar-B-Q. Quick's 7th St. Bar-B-Q, Wyandot Barbeque, Porky's Pit Bar-B-Q and Johnny's Bar-B-Q were all founded by former Rosedale employees. In 1954 Rieke set up his daughter, Marlynne, and her husband in the barbecue business. They operated Merriam Barbeque for 30 years.

Barbecue pretty much became Anthony Rieke's life.

"My wife told me I'm married to the barbecue," he once admitted. "I'd come down here about 5:30 in the morning and I'd work till about 4 or so in the afternoon. Then most times I had to come back in the evening."

And that's the way it was right up until the end.

It's hard to walk away from something you've built yourself. Built from nothing. Even after he had supposedly retired, Anthony Rieke would keep going to the restaurant to make sure things were running smoothly. He'd check out the wood supply. He'd check out the books. There wasn't anything about Rosedale Bar-B-Q that he didn't know or care about.

"If I saw I could improve it in any way, I would do it," he said. "I just always had ideas how things could be better."

Anthony Rieke died Wednesday March 5, 1997. He was 92.

RICH DAVIS
THE VISIONARY

Every time somebody somewhere plucks a bottle of K.C. Masterpiece barbecue sauce off the grocery shelf and plunks it in the cart, at some subliminal level Kansas City is positively associated with barbecue. For that reason, Rich Davis, more than anyone else except Calvin Trillin, is responsible for perpetuating our national reputation as a barbecue capital.

Rich Davis is something of a renaissance man. In his first career he was a family and child psychologist. In his second career, he created arguably the most successful line of barbecue sauces ever. Then he launched a chain of popular barbecue restaurants. Then he returned to the kitchen to make more sauces, marinades and salad dressings. He's a poet. He's a community leader. And he's a really nice guy.

Once Rich Davis boldly put forth a $200 million plan to build an Epcot Center-style tourist attraction here in Kansas City to be called Food World, or something like that. The purpose of this visionary theme park would have been to celebrate Kansas City's role as food capital of the planet.

Creativity has been Rich Davis' hallmark.

It was in the late 1970s that he created his now worldfamous sauce, K.C. Masterpiece.

"I barbecued all my life," Davis says. "My dad taught me how to barbecue when I was a kid. And of course we barbecued with our young families in the '50s and '60s. In those days there really were no good commercial barbecue sauces. I kept fiddling around until I came up with something I really liked."

He sold his sauce business in 1986, and Rich got rich.

Meanwhile he started the K.C. Masterpiece restaurant empire which, in 2001, was purchased by Famous Dave's of America Inc., a Minnesota-based developer and franchiser of barbecue eateries and blues clubs.

From time to time an elitist food critic will visit one of the K.C. Masterpiece restaurants and pronounce it "bland" or "tame" or somehow less than "authentic." A careful reading between the lines of these reviews reveals that the restaurants are actually being damned for not being Arthur Bryant's.

This is fundamentally unfair. It's like blaming a chicken for not being a pig. K.C. Masterpiece is what it is: a clean, well-lighted place with consistently good food served by a friendly, well-trained wait staff.

You can't imitate Bryant's. Anybody who tried would be justifiably excoriated by the aforementioned critics.

The barbecue family is a big one. Brother Rich may not be as old or as gritty as brother Arthur, but he has his strengths. He has, for one, initiated many first-time visitors into the world of Kansas City barbecue. If it weren't for K.C. Masterpiece and its accessibility, many tourists and even residents, for that matter, would never know the pleasures of a slow-smoked hunk of meat. Once they've tasted it, you know they'll love it. And maybe next time they'll venture forth and try other places. And that's good for everybody.

Rich Davis has been an evangelist for Kansas City barbecue. He's been responsible for thousands of converts over the last two decades. His creative mind, visionary spirit and entrepreneurial efforts have helped consolidate our claim to the world's best barbecue.

BILARDO: THE NAME LIVES ON

The name Bilardo is familiar to lovers of big band music in Kansas City. Vince Bilardo Sr., a popular bandleader and drummer, has entertained crowds of jazz fans for a generation. For the last decade the Bilardo family's name has also become well-known to barbecue lovers through its line of barbecue sauces, rubs and salsas.

The Bilardos entered barbecue sauce competitions as a hobby in the mid-1980s, and in 1987 one of their sauces won the Great Lenexa Barbeque Battle.

In 1993 they decided their products were good enough to go public, so they formed a company to manufacture and market their wares. Eventually, Bilardo products were sold in more than 100 area grocery stores and 200 other outlets nationwide. Problem was, the family members involved in making and selling the sauce all had regular "day jobs," and as the sauce biz became more successful it outgrew the family's capacity to run it.

So, in order to keep the brand viable The Bilardos sold their company to a competitor, Original Juan Specialty Foods Inc. of Kansas City, Kansas.

"We want to be like Kraft, with different labels," says Joe Polo, president of Original Juan. "We want to grow our product lines and acquire companies that have a national or regional reputation. It gives us more diversity, so if one line isn't doing well one year it helps balance out the income."

"We wanted to get the brand into a larger food company, where it could grow and live on," Vince Bilardo Jr. says. "We've worked with five different co-packers in the food business over eight years. Original Juan's operation is far and away the best operation we've dealt with."

Original Juan's labels include the Fiesta line; Pain Is Good/The Sultans of Sizzle hot sauces and salsas; and Original Juan and Calido Chile Traders lines of salsas, marinades and barbecue sauces.

"We hope to piggyback on their products and penetrate that market," Polo says. "If you have a foothold, they are more likely to expand the line that you are carrying."

— Joyce Smith

BARBECUE
ENTREPRENEURS

Before K.C. Masterpiece there was glorified ketchup.

If fate had taken another turn, we might be slathering "muschup" - a mixture of dilled mustard and ketchup - on our ribs. Never heard of muschup? That's because Rich Davis' barbecue sauce took off first.

And nearly 20 years later, K.C. Masterpiece Barbecue Sauce is a national best-seller and continues to dominate the Kansas City market with more than a 50 percent share.

Thanks to a consuming passion for barbecue, Kansas City is awash in barbecue sauce. Dozens of local entrepreneurs are betting that they can take their sauce and duplicate Davis' success.

Exactly how many new sauces are introduced to this market each year is difficult to say, although barbecue aficionados insist there's enough out there that a barbecue enthusiast could sample a new sauce every weekend for a year and still not have tasted them all.

"When you go up and down the supermarket aisles in Kansas City, you find more tiny, beginning barbecue sauces in this city than I've seen in any other I've been to on my travels," says Davis.

At last count, Scott O'Meara had 430 bottles on display at his Overland Park barbecue restaurant. He estimates about 40 of them hail from Kansas City.

"It's amazing how many local guys there are," says O'Meara, who owns Boardroom Bar-B-Q restaurant.

"I'd say about 90 percent started in the barbecue contests, won a few ribbons and thought 'Hey, I ought to market a sauce.' "

FIRE AND CAPITAL

Ardie Davis has watched more than a few barbecue-hobbyists-turned-barbecue-entrepreneurs jump feet first into the sauce market and come up sputtering.

"They build up the Rich Davis legend as achievable for themselves. And it's a great story," admits Ardie Davis (who is no relation to Rich Davis), "but few people are going to achieve that."

Ardie Davis should know. He is the founder of the American Royal Barbecue Sauce Contest, which nets over 200 entries a year. The contest features commercially produced barbecue sauces from around the world.

So what makes a successful sauce? "You need a fire in your belly and capital," Davis says.

Kyle Bubeck, president of Adrian's Barbecue Sauce, knows a bit about capital. He has invested $1.5 million over three years and expects to spend another $50,000 to $75,000 to get his sauce on supermarket shelves in 25 to 30 states.

Like so many barbecue sauces, Adrian's was initially manufactured in his mother's kitchen and distributed to 10 gourmet shops. After buying the fledgling company from his brother, Bubeck moved to a 1,000-square-foot facility with a mixing tank. Next

pany from his brother, Bubeck moved to a 1,000-square-foot facility with a mixing tank. Next came a move to a facility with an automated bottling line. Since April, it has been distributed by a Chicago-based food processor.

Bubeck says an outside processor provided him with access to research facilities and better quality control. But to attract the attention of a broker who could get his product into supermarket warehouses, he had to spend the kind of money few hobbyists can afford.

"We found that the way we were able to get a broker was by tying ourselves to the Chiefs," Bubeck says. During the 1991-92 season, Bubeck spent $40,000 to be an official sponsor of the Kansas City Chiefs.

But if he had it to do over, Bubeck says he would spend the money on in-store promotions.

PEDDLING SAUCE

Carmen Sharp stops supermarket shoppers in their tracks by offering them sausage bits skewered on a toothpick. Each morsel swims in a sea of Jazzy Barbecue Sauce.

As soon as her potential customer pops the morsel in their mouth, Sharp launches into the story of her sauce, a 65-year-old recipe handed down to her from her grandmother.

Four years ago Sharp quit her job as an assistant manager of a restaurant and began marketing her sauce full-time. In the beginning she rented the kitchen at Westport Allen Center to make her sauce with the help of her daughter, then 12.

It would take them two days to pour and label each bottle by hand. When they had 50 cases, Sharp would load her car up and peddle her sauce to anyone who would try it. "I started with small neighborhood stores because I was scared that the supermarkets would say, 'We have Masterpiece and Gates. We don't want yours.'"

But she found that if she was willing to do in-store demos and take responsibility to keep their shelves stocked, many were willing to give her a foot in the door.

Even though Jazzy is no longer bottled by hand, Sharp admits it's still a struggle to make a living selling sauce.

"The bad part about being a one-man show is that I'm so bogged down in the day-to-day operations (that) I don't get to lead the company to new growth," says Sharp.

PIGS WILL FLY

Even if you have a great barbecue sauce, the chances of getting rich — to paraphrase Ardie Davis — are somewhat more remote than seeing a pig fly.

"I've seen a few that have a chance, but I would characterize most as not making a lot of money," says Davis.

To help aspiring entrepreneurs decide if they have the right stuff, Davis put together a series of articles titled "Selling Sauce," which was initially published in The Bullsheet, the Kansas City Barbeque Society's monthly newsletter.

As Davis scans the supermarket shelves for up-and-coming trends in barbecue sauce, he criticizes a tendency to rely on the tried-and-true tomato-based sauce. ▶

tendency to rely on the tried-and-true tomato-based sauce.

Perhaps it's a measure of comfort, but the majority of Kansas City-based entrepreneurs continue to model their sauces on the familiar tastes of such legendary barbecue restaurants as Arthur Bryant's and Gates & Sons.

"We're stuck in a rut," says Davis. "Everyone tends to think of tomato-based sauces. I think there's room for departure from that with more vinegar and fruit-based sauces."

"It does seem like most of the sauces are somewhat similar," says O'Meara, who features a "Sauce of the Month" promotion at his restaurant. "You won't find anything vinegar- or mustard-based, like in the Carolinas. They all resemble Masterpiece and Gates in certain respects, but it's amazing what little twists are out there."

And chances are, with K.C. Masterpiece's introduction of "non-red" sauces including its Honey Dijon and Honey Teriyaki flavors, a spate of honey-flavored barbecue sauces may not be far behind.

A SOPHISTICATE PALATE

Karen Putnam stirs a 60-gallon steel vat of her popular raspberry-flavored barbecue sauce. Yes, raspberry.

"I wanted something that was totally different and away from what everyone else was doing. I like raspberries, so I put them in," says Putnam, a professional chef and caterer who markets her own Flower of the Flames Raspberry Barbecue Sauce.

In Kansas City barbecue circles, Putnam is known as the "guruette" of sauce. She has won hundreds of awards and has helped a number of competing sauces get a start.

The Flower of the Flames line includes seven products – three barbecue sauces, a barbecue salsa, a dry rub, a poultry marinade and a mild-flavored kids barbecue sauce - which are available through local gourmet shops, supermarkets and mail-order.

Two years ago Putnam moved production into a commercial kitchen nestled in a Lenexa industrial park. She sublets the kitchen facility for $115 per day, plus supplies. If an aspiring sauce entrepreneur wants her help with recipe research and development, she charges anywhere from $45 to $50 an hour.

"When we started out we didn't know anything. If we can save people time and errors," she shrugs, "why not?"

Dick Pope isn't worried about local competition either.

Outside of K.C. Masterpiece, the only barbecue sauce that commands a significant share of the market is Gates & Sons. Pope, a partner in Saucemaster's Gourmet Foods, which markets Old K.C. Barbeque Sauce, says Kansas City consumers are eager to support a wide array of locally produced barbecue sauces.

Says Pope, "It's a market where I don't look at other sauces so much as competition as I do a part of the barbecue scene."

— Jill Silva

PLAYING WITH THE BIG BOYS

Duane Roberts has turned a kitchen concoction into gold.

In the beginning Roberts just wanted to make barbecue sauce for his family. At home after work, Roberts tinkered with ketchup. He added and subtracted flavors, trying to get the right taste and texture. It took more than a year, but Roberts finally got the taste he wanted. He called it Pit Boss barbecue sauce.

"I'm kind of obsessive about things," he said. "We were just trying to make the best barbecue sauce we could, and it kind of took over."

He decided to compete in the big leagues of grocery store retailing.

Getting it made in large quantities was the next step. Health departments frown on businesses that sell homemade food products, so Roberts and his wife rented a commercial kitchen in Lenexa.

"We went to Sam's Club and bought all the stuff and hauled it out there. It took about 12 hours one day to cook, bottle, label and seal it," Roberts said. The effort produced 40 cases of barbecue sauce. Ashley Roberts made the rounds at grocery stores, talking to managers and doing a few product demonstrations.

"It's been a lot of fun and it's still fun, but it turned out to be a lot more work than we thought at first," she said.

Roberts' sauce has finished 14th out of 264 entries in the American Royal's Best Sauce on the Planet competition, and fifth out of 99 entries in the Mild Tomato category.

As demand for the product has grown, so have the challenges. Sauce ingredients were easy to get, but Roberts learned ketchup is too expensive to use as a sauce base. Now the sauce is made with tomato paste, water and vinegar instead.

He also had to get bottles, seals, a nutrition statement and a bar code, all from different places. Packaging and distribution became increasingly important.

"We decided we needed something more professional-looking than the labels I made in the home computer," Roberts said.

Now everything is cooked, bottled, sealed and labeled by a contract bottler. A commercial artist designed the labels and a distributor gets the product on grocery shelves.

"What sells it is the character in the bottle," said Kevin Pereira of Palmentere Brothers of Kansas City, Roberts' distributor for the past year.

Roberts has since developed a meat rub. Both products are doing well, but Roberts said he's not ready to give up his day job running an ice-machine rental business.

"We'll see what happens," he said. "It's starting to simmer, and maybe someday it will come to a full boil."

— John Heuertz

EAT IT AND BEAT IT

LIL' JAKE'S

The Kansas City Star has produced some fine barbecue writing over the years, some of which appears in this section. One of my favorite pieces of Q-prose is this 1998 profile of Lil' Jake's by one of my favorite people, *Star Magazine* writer/editor Tim Engle.

A faded pink concrete pig stands guard outside the place — the place with a name that's equal parts invitation and warning: EAT IT AN' BEAT IT.

And if you happen to be driving through this neck of the woods, 13th and Grand, with the car window rolled down, you're a goner. You're highly likely to take 'em up on the invitation part. The aroma of hickory smoke is intoxicating.

Erick Roeder, a young Kansas City lawyer, knows all this. It's only been a year and some months since he concluded, as he was motoring past one day, that Lil'

Jake's Eat It An' Beat It barbecue was the sort of place where he wanted to be a regular.

"It just looked kind of cool," he says. "It almost looks like it's from another era." So these days Roeder, 27, is indeed a Lil' Jake's regular. One of his favorites is a "Southern-style" sandwich: pork topped with coleslaw topped with sauce. He and friend or two friends or seven or eight friends — mostly a group that went to law school together in Columbia — are there every week for lunch, usually on Thursdays.

Their hangout is a Kansas City institution, a place

much beloved by a lot of folks and, in a town heralded for its barbecue, a keeper of the flame.

Of the dozens of places in Kansas City that serve barbecue, many must be called restaurants. Lil' Jake's, however, is a *joint*.

For one thing, it's tiny. *T'-nee*. The walls inside are pink. Pink-pink. The floor is black-and-white checkerboard. Brownies tempt from under glass, not far from the potato salad container where customers toss in their business cards hoping to win the "slab of the month." Ribs and chicken occupy a warmer behind the

Eat-in sandwiches come in paper boats; beans and potato salad and coleslaw come with the spoon stuck in it.

Erick Roeder's pal John Nesbitt, 26, who for about a year always ordered the same lunch, started straying to other menu items. Then one day recently he told a waitress he was going 'old school' — and she promptly said, "Rib sandwich, side of baked beans and a medium Dr Pepper?"

He thought that was pretty cool.

One regular customer always grabs a pad and writes his own order (although he doesn't know the shorthand: "B" for beef, "T" for turkey, etc.) and runs a tab.

Outside, Lil' Jake's is an island in a sea of cars. Heck, if you didn't know better, you'd think PARK HERE was its name.

There's a story there. Danny Edwards, Lil' Jake's affable 43-year-old proprietor, says the Lil' brick building he leased in 1983 (and purchased four years later) used to be the office for the parking lots that lap it on three sides. Directly across Grand Boulevard, the fourth side, are more cars, the Town Pavilion's parking garage.

The name Jake Edwards is legendary in Kansas City barbecue lore. Jake, Danny's dad, died in 1984, and although there's still a barbecue restaurant that bears his name, the Edwards family isn't part of it.

Danny Edwards says his dad learned the art of Texas barbecue in the Dallas-Fort Worth area. In 1938 Jake Edwards opened his first "Old Southern Pit" restaurant here at 1018 Baltimore Ave., across from what would later become Macy's. By 1960 he had five barbecue joints, all downtown.

By the time Danny was 11 he was working as a busboy at one of his dad's places; at 17 he learned how to cook; at 24, Danny took over the original space at 10th and Baltimore, and renamed it Lil' Jake's.

That was in 1980. Edwards was there until 1984, when, he says, his voice dripping sarcasm the way some of his customers drip sauce, "the city kicked me out so they could build a real nice parking garage."

That's when he moved to 1227 Grand.

As for "Eat It An' Beat It" — well, remember how we said the place is, uh, cozy? The "dining room" contains two counterlike tables with eight stools apiece. There are two more stools "up front" — we're talking maybe 10 steps from the door — at the real counter. The congestion eases in warm weather, when Jake's offers al fresco dining.

Maximum seating capacity inside: 18 people. Then there are the hungry people lined up for takeout - and those who would like to be off their feet but have to wait for someone to get up.

"You eat your lunch and you get on down the road," Edwards explains. "Because the seat you relinquish may be your own someday when you're waiting for a seat." Karma, Kansas City-style.

The Lil' Jake's staff, however — that'd be Edwards and four employees — are no barbecue Nazis.

Legend has it that there was a mean waitress once upon a time who wasn't shy about telling customers to hit the bricks ...

"That could've been my second wife, Diane," Edwards says with a broad grin. Diane, he mentions later, was trained by his first wife, Maureen, who sometimes would come to work in costume - like as the wisecracking waitress Flo from the old TV show "Alice." *Kiss mah grits!*

Annnnnn-yway, if one of the waitresses at Lil' Jake's delivers a lid with your third refill of coffee, you should realize she's trying to tell you something.

You're done eating, buddy. Now beat it. And have a good day.

Back behind the counter, in "the box" where Danny Edwards deftly slices beef brisket and turkey and ham

for sandwiches and where the phone's always ringing and the back door's always opening from someone's trip out to the pits - well, if it weren't for frequent "Right behind you's," the place would resemble a Three Stooges movie. It's tight.

It's not quite as bad out in the dining room, but the scarcity of space brings us to another of Lil' Jake's charms: More often than not, you have to sit beside a stranger. You may even end up *talking* to that person.

It's Lil' Jake's version of communal dining, that oh-so-European tradition that's reportedly trendy again in places like New York.

But these impromptu encounter groups can have delightful results. Here's how it might go: You stop by for lunch (Lil' Jake's is open only for lunch, till 2:30) with two co-workers. "Grab a seat and I'll get your order in just a sec," one of the waitresses says. That'd be either Rachel Donelson or Becky Gould.

Scanning the room, you quickly ascertain that the grabbin's good only at Table 1, we'll call it. On one side the stools are occupied-occupied-empty-empty; on the other it's empty-empty-empty-occupied.

This puts the three of you across from, it turns out, a twentysomething couple just off the train from St. Louis. It's spring break. She's in college; he's not; they're planning to crash at his aunt's house, although, he admits, he hasn't talked to this aunt in some time.

Donelson — Danny's 18-year-old goddaughter, who worked here a couple of summers in high school and since graduation last year — says not everyone takes to small talk with strangers. When customers "zigzag themselves," it can make finding seats together difficult.

But she and Gould do what they can to get conversations rolling, which can be as simple as asking someone if they work nearby or what brought them to town.

"You really can't sit and eat in silence when it's really packed," she says.

So what you get at Lil' Jake's are conversations like the one Harvey Bodker had the other day with a fellow from the U.S. attorney's office. Bodker, who owns a real estate firm, asked the lawyer if he ever watched the D.A. drama "Michael Hayes" on TV. No, he replied. Well, Bodker said, his son, a surgeon, never watches "ER" either.

"You're this close - how can you not talk?" Bodker asks. "This is the place to be friendly."

—Tim Engle

THE GREAT

BARBECUE MISSION

Here's a great barbecue tale from 1995 by one of *The Kansas City Star's* best barbecue writers, Jim Fussell.

—D.W.

Harold Mintz had a meaty problem on his hands.

The trunk of his rental car was crammed so full of meat he was having a hard time getting it closed.

There it was in all its glory: 18 slabs of ribs, 8 pounds of sliced beef, ham, pork, turkey, sausage, lamb, chicken, burnt ends - not to mention buckets of beans, oceans of sauce, cups, menus, napkins and a dizzying array of other barbecue bric-a-brac.

"This isn't going to work," he said, rearranging the sumptuous-smelling packages in the parking lot of Jack Fiorella's Smoke Stack of Martin City — one of nine Kansas City barbecue restaurants he visited on a rollicking one-day tour of local barbecue haunts. "How am I going to get all this home?"

But it was going to work. It had to work. Because he was on a quest, a holy mission, really. And more than 40 friends back home in Washington, D.C., were depending on him to haul the good stuff back so they could party in style.

How did he get himself in such a pickle?

It started with a free frequent-flier ticket that was about to expire.

Mintz, executive director of a trade-show display company in Springfield, Va., decided he'd give the ticket to his wife, Susan, so she could visit a friend in Arizona. But before she could schedule the trip, her friend moved to Las Vegas. Susan Mintz didn't want to go to Las Vegas.

So Harold got another idea. He decided he would travel to a city famous for its food, buy some, and then fly it back to Washington and have a gigantic party.

Good idea, his wife thought.

The only questions: Where to go, and what to get?

Maine lobsters? Too expensive.

Chicago steaks? Too boring.

And then it came to him - barbecue.

But what kind — North Carolina had good barbecue. As did Memphis.

And Texas.

"Of course!" Mintz finally thought. "Kansas City!"

And so it was that Mintz on Friday flew to Kansas City, with just one goal - to take home the most marvelous, mouth-watering, spine-straightening, drop-dead delicious barbecue anywhere on this or any other planet - Kansas City barbecue.

At 6 feet 5 inches and 210 pounds, with dark, salty black hair and chiseled features, he looks like a cross between actor Tom Selleck and the late musician Frank Zappa. Possessed of a New York-style gregariousness that was at once charming, genuine and bold, he didn't waste much time picking the natives' brains about barbecue.

"So, mister driver," he said. "You're from around here, aren't you? What's your favorite barbecue?"

"I go to Gates," the driver said. "And Hayward's."

Good, Mintz thought. Those were already on his list of planned places to visit.

His first scheduled stop: Ricky's Pit barbecue in Kansas City, Kan. As he drove, he laughed at the tongue-tingling tanginess of the day to come.

"Ha-haa! We're on a mission from God!" he said, borrowing a

line from the Blues Brothers movie. "I should have sunglasses and it should be dark outside."

Suddenly, on the way to Ricky's, he spied something out of the corner of his eye.

"Oh, what's this?" he screamed, practically slamming on the brakes. It was the Hickory Log barbecue. And even though it wasn't on his list, he just couldn't resist one little peek.

"I gotta take a picture," he said. He blasted out of the car like a nitro-fired rocket, camera flailing wildly from its strap. He flagged down a car.

"Is this a good place?" he asked.

"This is the best," the customer said.

"What did you all get?"

And so it went. His trek started at 11 a.m. It didn't end until the sun went down. When it was all over, he had driven 153 miles straight through the heart of "Barbecueville" and spent more than $400 on food alone, even though he got some of it for nothing.

Outside the Smoke Stack, Mintz continued to repack his aromatic trunk. The momentary frustration of how to get it all home quickly faded.

"Right now, life is good, my friend," he said. "Life is more than good. Life is excellent. Can't you smell me? I smell like barbecue and smoke. And my mustache is a little dirty. But that's all right. That's good."

It was 8 p.m., time to head home. But before heading back to his hotel, Mintz just had to immortalize a piece of Kansas City's barbecue culture on film one last time.

"Oh, man," he said, scrambling out of the car to take a picture of an only-in-Kansas-City sign that brought a smile to his face.

The sign read in part: "We accept food stamps" and "Barbecue pig ear snouts."

"Perfect," he said under his breath. "Perfect."

—Jim Fussell

46 THE GRAND BARBECUE:
BARBECUE CAPITAL

Harold and Susan Mintz and a friend celebrate the successful conclusion of Harold's barbecue mission.

GRACE HARRIS

AMAZIN'

God gives you a gift, Grace Harris says with all the righteous confidence in the world. "God gives us all something that we can make a living on. And some people are cooks."

Indeed.

God gave Grace Harris the gift of barbecue cooking. And to taste Grace Harris' barbecue is to understand that some gifts are greater than others. Grace's barbecue is, like the sign says, amazing.

Grace Harris has been serving barbecue at Kansas City's Grand Emporium ever since the nationally renowned nightclub opened in 1985. Club founder Roger Naber says it was a natural choice. "The kind of music we wanted to feature here, blues, roots rock, jazz, it all just fits with barbecue. They go together. And Grace is as good at what she does as the musicians who play here are at what they do."

Grace accepts the compliment but is quick to point out "I was doing this stuff long before there was a Grand Emporium."

Naber agrees. "That's why we wanted Grace. She already had a reputation."

Grace has been dishing up barbecue with a side of blues for a while now.

She was born Grace Washington in 1940 in Carroll County, Mississippi. But it was in Louisiana, where her family eventually moved, where her love of blues and barbecue was born.

"During those days, there was a limitation of where black people went," Harris says. "So (neighbors) would have a little hole in the ground, put a rod in it and barbecue. They would go from house to house, play the blues and dance until day. The only way you know about the blues is having lived it."

When Grace was 14 years old her family moved, to Kansas City. Her grandfather operated a nightclub here called Fancy Dancing on Quindaro, and Grace loved the atmosphere of the place. The camaraderie between the musicians. The way the music made people happy. She decided then that music was always going to be a part of her life.

Later, when she went to work for Otis Boyd at his barbecue restaurant, Boyd 'N' Son, she acquired the skills and secrets to perfect her God-given gift, and before long she was practicing those secrets and skills for some of the best musicians in the world.

"Blues and barbecue, it's a love thing," Harris says. "I love to give these musicians this barbecue because it's what they love. They love to give me this blues because that's what I love."

NO ORDINARY JOE

OKLAHOMA JOE'S

When Jeff Stehney wanted to open a barbecue *joint* — not a restaurant — he knew he was at a disadvantage, because it's as hard for an affluent young white guy from the suburbs to open and operate an *authentic* barbecue joint, as it is for an affluent young white guy from the suburbs to sing the blues. It's not impossible. But it is hard.

So what he did was locate his establishment between a gas station and a liquor store. Then, instead of offering table service, he made folks line up at a counter to order their food. Then he nailed sheets of corrugated tin on the walls. And finally he made some of the best barbecue Kansas Citians have ever tasted.

"You have to be *real* good to succeed in the barbecue business in Kansas City," Stehney understates. "In this town, people will drive right by a perfectly adequate barbecue establishment on their way to their favorite joint. You don't get that in other food categories."

Stehney's joint is called Oklahoma Joe's and it's at 47th and Mission. He opened the place in 1996 with a partner, Joe Davidson, whose nick-name is (you guessed it) Oklahoma Joe. Davidson, who also developed a well-known line of wood smokers, has since sold his interest in the restaurant to Stehney. Stehney now runs the place with his wife, Joy.

Most, if not all, of the hundreds of cookers active on the barbecue competition circuit dream of one day winning the American Royal

Barbecue. Most, if not all, of them also dream of starting their own restaurant. Jeff Stehney has realized both dreams.

In 1993, after competing for just two seasons, Stehney's team "Slaughterhouse Five" won the Royal.

"We were absolutely *dominant* that year," he recalls. "We entered 23 events and came away with *eight* grand championships.

"My personal breakthrough in barbecue, however, was the year before when I entered the World Brisket Open in Texas as an individual competitor. I won first *and* second place and $6,000."

Brisket is now the bestseller at Oklahoma Joe's, though Stehney points out that his pulled pork sandwich is also pretty darn good.

Over 400 people a day crowd into the 70-seat joint. His success has prompted Stehney to consider opening a second restaurant, and he has retained the services of a franchise attorney.

"We're doin' something right," he says. "If you give people championship-caliber barbecue, they'll come back."

Joy and Jeff Stehney at their joint.

L.C.RICHARDSON

HEIR APPARENT

What does L.C. Richardson think of the buzz that his joint is "the next place to be" for barbecue connoisseurs, just as Arthur Bryant's was 20 years ago?

"Oh," he says in an unwearied tone. "I've heard it, but it's not for me to say. It could be accurate, sure. But I'm on my side, you know."

Richardson is just happy to be smelling those slow-smoked ribs cooking in his own place. And he won't argue with any word-of-mouth that sends more people to his door. That he ever opened a joint of his own attests to the fact that Richardson won't let opportunity pass by.

In 1986, while he was working as a chef for Farmland Industries, the company began to reduce its workforce by offering early retirement and severance packages. For some it was a time of uncertainty and stress.

"It was a blessing at the time for me," Richardson says. "It supplied me with the money I wouldn't have had on my own."

He opened his restaurant on Blue Parkway in a building shared with a liquor store. Another opportunity seized. The location worked so well, in fact, he later bought the store and turned it into a dining area.

"Being next to the liquor store was good help for me," he says. "They'd come out and smell that cooking and, you know, they couldn't resist."

It seems once folks taste L.C.'s fare, they spread the word. Now celebrities drop by for a taste. Tourists, too. And a second restaurant recently opened in Lenexa, on 95th St.

Richardson has come a long way from the backyard where he first started cooking as a kid.

"I can't remember my first barbecue," he says. "I can't remember a time when I didn't have barbecue."

Born in Mississippi, Richardson learned the virtues of slow cooking early on. But barbecue is not his only culinary skill. After arriving in Kansas City in 1953, Richardson began his education in kitchens all over Kansas City.

He cooked everything from down-home meals at the Wishbone Restaurant to fine entrees and pastries for patrons of area hotels and executives at Farmland. He believes he could have opened a restaurant with anything on the menu.

"I chose barbecue because it was so important in Kansas City," Richardson says. "I did it so maybe I could stick around."

— Michael Humphrey
is a freelance writer
in Kansas City

A Fiorella family barbecue restaurant is a relaxing and enjoyable place to be. One gets the sense, however, that a Fiorella family reunion might be a different story.

The Fiorella family is to Kansas City barbecue what the Ewing family of the TV show "Dallas" was to Texas oil. Industrious and fractious.

While one hopes that it's true that the family that prays together stays together, it doesn't appear to be true that this family that once barbecued together is glued together.

There are actually as many barbecue establishments in the Kansas City area owned by Fiorellas as by Gateses. The difference is that the Gates empire is a single company. At last count there were in the Kansas City metropolitan region six Fiorella barbecue restaurants, owned by five Fiorella siblings, operated by four separate and distinct Fiorella companies.

A few generations back the Fiorellas were farmers in Jackson County. But when the agriculture economy went bad during the Depression, the family got into the grocery business, and for years that paid the bills. Then, in the 1950s, national supermarket chains began to move into the area and the Fiorellas found it hard to compete. That's when Russell Fiorella Sr., whose children now own the various Smoke Stack and Jack's Stack eateries in town, decided to make the move from butcher to barbecue maker.

The original Smoke Stack is the one on Hickman Mills Drive (South U.S. 71 highway) and for a while it was not just the family business, it was the family home. When they first opened the place, the Fiorellas moved from their 23-room house in Brookside into a six-room apartment above the restaurant.

Russell's son Jack, now 59, remembers customers banging on the apartment door demanding barbecue after the restaurant had closed for the night.

Jack and his siblings worked evenings and weekends at the place, waiting tables, washing dishes and tending the pit. That's how they learned the business. Each of them. Individually.

Two of Russell's daughters, Carol Fiorella and Diane Fiorella Marak, now own and operate the original restaurant.

Another sibling, Mary Fiorella McPheron, owns the Smoke Stack on Wornall Road.

And Russell Fiorella Jr. owns the Smoke Stack on North Church Road, near Liberty.

A visit to any of these joints provides ample evidence that these Fiorella siblings learned the barbecue business quite well.

Then there's Jack.

Here's a story about Jack Fiorella: On July 1, 1963, when he was 21 years old, he was slicing barbecue at the restaurant. It was raining hard

Left: Diners enjoy their barbecue at Fiorella's Jack Stack in the Freighthouse near Union Station. Above right: Pitmaster Chris Dorman wrestles ribs at the 95th street restaurant.

outside. Not that he noticed much. He was pretty busy. Suddenly a bolt of lightning struck a neon sign on the restaurant, traveled through the building's electrical system and jumped right out of the meat cutter and into Jack.

Obviously he recovered. But you gotta wonder if maybe that jolt didn't do something to the man. He crackles with energy and big ideas. He flashes with passion.

Jack Fiorella owns the Jack's Stack Barbecue restaurants in Martin City, in Overland Park and downtown in the historic Freight House.

"I've always seen ways of making things better," Fiorella says. And that's exactly what led to his leaving the family company.

"My father was lenient with letting me try new things at the restaurant, but it got to be a little bit of a fight," Fiorella recalls. So with Russell Sr.'s help, Jack went off to Martin City, where he set up his own operation.

Whether Jack's different approach to business created tension in the family or whether tension in the family was what made Jack want to strike out on his own is probably impossible to know. The Fiorellas probably don't even know.

And, frankly, it's really none of our business.

Jack Fiorella kept using the Smoke Stack name at the Martin City place, even while the rest of the family continued using it as well in their individual and collective enterprises.

This created problems that came to a head when Jack Fiorella decided to open a second restaurant.

"I was told (by family members) that I was not allowed to use the name," Fiorella says. "So I decided to call it Fiorella's Jack Stack Bar-B-Q.

Jack Fiorella's barbecue establishments aren't joints. They're restaurants. The kind of restaurants any Chamber of Commerce staffer would be proud to recommend to a visitor from out of town.

In 1996 Fiorella was named Restaurateur of the Year by the Greater Kansas City Restaurant Association. The award recognizes quality of operation, and an owner's leadership ability and involvement in the restaurant industry and community.

"Jack is very dedicated and very quality-oriented, making sure that every plate comes out well," says Carl Degen, executive vice president of the Missouri Restaurant Association. "He takes barbecue dining to another level."

Now, whether or not barbecue dining actually needs to be taken to another level, and if it does, what that level should look like is a question open to debate. But the proposition that Jack Fiorella's restaurants are not typical within the barbecue biz is not debatable.

Check out his menu.

First of all there's things like blackened chicken breasts, rack of lamb and porterhouse steaks. And one summer, customers — excuse me, *diners* — at Jack's Stack could actually choose ostrich steaks if they wanted to.

Then — and this is the most shocking thing of all — there's a healthy helping of seafood on the menu. Fresh seafood. *Good* seafood.

At most barbecue joints the closest you'll get to seafood is when the Neanderthal in line next to you grunts, "I see food. I eat food."

These innovative additions to the Jack's Stack bill of fare are indicative of Jack Fiorella's restaurateurial restlessness.

He remembers a conversation with his wife, Delores, that prompted him to undertake one particular improvement campaign. "We were making a living," Fiorella says. "We were comfortable. Then my wife made the comment, 'We're a typical barbecue in a town known for its barbecue. We're good, but so is everybody else.' And that really aggravated me."

The two of them then came up with the idea of adding fresh fish grilled over hickory wood to their menu — something you're unlikely to see at Arthur Bryant's any time soon.

But then there's no record of Arthur Bryant ever having been hit by lightning.

"The old rule is that if something is successful, don't change it," Fiorella says. "That's always been a hard rule for me to live by."

THE MAN FROM HOPE

HAYWARD SPEARS

T here is a visionary from Hope, Arkansas, and he doesn't know a darn thing about White Houses or Whitewater. He does know about barbecue, smoked just like his dad taught him back on the farm.

Hayward Spears left Hope in 1954, but Hope never left him.

"I owe everything to my father," he says. "He was my role model. I remember him putting up the chicken and pork in the smokehouse. And he used to roast a whole pig in his pit for the Fourth of July. That left an impression on me."

Spears started cooking while still employed by GM and eventually opened a barbecue restaurant in 1972 on 95th and Antioch. His next big step in the barbecue biz was a risky one. You might even say it was visionary.

"When I moved out to College Boulevard back in 1981, it was probably the biggest gamble I ever took," Spears said. "Now it seems like it's the center of activity and some people think I'm a genius. I'm far from that."

Spears has come a long way from his Arkansas beginnings – just like that other famous man from, Hope. And his days of cooking at his restaurant have passed. As his son Hayward Spears, Jr. takes on more responsibility, Spears, Sr. says he has taken on a new role at his business.

"I meddle all day long now," he said. "That's my profession. I'm a well-seasoned meddler."

—Michael Humphrey

LINDSAY SHANNON

KANSAS CITY SPIRIT

T ens of thousands of Kansas City kids have grown up in this town oblivious to its two great cultural traditions, blues and barbecue.

But not Lindsay Shannon.

"In the '50s, I would tune my radio to all the blues stations. The blues just got to me," says Shannon, a graduate of Southwest High School in Kansas City.

When he was a kid he'd go to ballgames at old Municipal Stadium, passing a host of barbecue joints on the way. Eventually he learned to appreciate each establishment for its unique personality: Deluxe Bar-B-Q had its heaping sandwiches; Dixie Lan had its tangy, spicy sauces; and Harris Bar-B-Q had its fiery sauce.

"Blues and barbecue became the two main passions in my life," Shannon says.

After college, a stint in the Air Force and jobs in Pennsylvania, New Jersey and Iowa, he ended up back home in Kansas City in 1971. He worked for a while in radio and outdoor advertising.

But his soul wasn't satisfied.

In 1977, Shannon started putting together blues shows on Kansas City radio stations, starting with KCUR-FM, then KCFX-FM. And in spite of Kansas City's rich heritage as a blues town,

Shannon's program was for years one of the few places on the radio dial where one could tune in to the blues.

"The whole time I was doing my radio show, I found myself talking to my listeners about barbecuing," Shannon recalls. "I'd say things like 'You should turn your radio up loud because the blues, as they waft across the meat, will make it taste that much better.' It got to be fun to talk about barbecue, blues, beer and baseball... all these B's. I would talk about how the 'B's are buzzing tonight.'

"So I was headed in a direction. It became clearer over time what I should do."

Finally, in 1990, at the corner of 85th and Troost, Lindsay Shannon found his calling and fulfilled his destiny. It was then and there that he, and his wife Jo, established their roadhouse, B.B.'s Lawnside Bar-B-Q.

Timothy Finn, The Star's pop music writer and former restaurant critic, described B.B.'s as "the kind of place where a regular walks through the door and a cold beer is waiting for him by the time he gets to the bar."

It's also the kind of place where some of the nation's best acoustic blues acts perform enveloped in the aroma of some of Kansas City's best barbecue.

While Roger Naber's Grand Emporium has provided a venue for electrified blues, Shannon's joint has emphasized the unplugged variety.

Both serve outstanding barbecue.

Together they are the heart and soul of Kansas City tradition.

The spirit of barbecue is to make do with what you've got and celebrate that you've got it. The spirit of the blues is that, no matter what life throws your way, you survive and you sing about it. These kindred spirits are alive and well at B.B.'s Lawnside. Though Shannon admits that keeping them alive has sometimes been a challenge.

"We've had some times when we couldn't pay the bills," he recalls. "We'd sit at home and wonder, 'Are we going to have to sell the house? Are we going to have to auction off the kids?' But somehow we found a way, and that's all you can do."

★ ★ ★ ★ ★ ★ ★ ★ ★

FILLING STATION

BARBECUE ODYSSEY

Some are called to cook. Others are called to eat. The former are called pitmasters. The latter are called guys with gas. Make that G.A.S. As in Gastronomic Appreciation Society.

The Gastronomic Appreciation Society is an amiable group of suburban white guys from Johnson County who've made it their collective mission in life to sample barbecue at every barbecue joint in the Kansas City metro area. As of this writing, they've visited about half of 'em.

As a public service G.A.S. has created a Web site on which members have posted reviews of the establishments they've tried. Some fellows in Florida happened upon said site and were inspired to visit Kansas City on a barbecue odyssey. After their visit they wrote a letter of thanks to their G.A.S. mentors. Here it is.

—D.W.

Dear G.A.S. Guys,

We know you'll be surprised to hear this, but you are worshiped as a minor deity by five strangers from afar. By "you," of course, we mean your Web site. And, as homage to your extensive research, we're pleased to offer this far-too-lengthy account of five out-of-towners and their recent journey for good Kansas City barbecue. Please feel free to post our intrepid report on your site.

Maybe we should explain who "we" are. We are a group of fools who have, for the most part, grown up together or lived together or otherwise come to enjoy each other's company in and around Florida.

Two years ago, looking for an excuse to get away from our wives, our girlfriends or both, we formed an annual guys-only weekend to discuss questionable business ideas, make bad jokes and eat good food. For reasons not worth explaining, we call it "The Summit of Love." After Atlanta in 1998 and Melbourne, Fla., in 1999, we chose Kansas City as our meeting place for 2000, because it offered barbecue, baseball and an REO Speedwagon/Styx concert all in one weekend, June 9-11.

FRIDAY, JUNE 9

We arrived in town around lunchtime, and our first stop was Gates on Main Street downtown because it was near the hotel. It smelled great from the parking lot. And then there were those waitresses hollering, "Hi! May I help you?" (Do they get special "annoying voice" training?)

Anyway, Gates got mixed reviews. Service was slow. Slaw was spicy. Beans were tasty, though. We all had ribs and we rated them average. They were a little dry. Only one of us appreciated the white bread under the meat.

After the Friday night Royals game, we looked desperately for a late-night barbecue joint to sample. We found only Gates was open.

Our belief is that a true major-league city should have several midnight barbecue options available. Please work with the convention and visitors association to rectify this state of affairs.

SATURDAY, JUNE 10

We all agreed your description of The Filling Station made it the best place to stop for lunch. But we were unprepared for the lovely site of a Dairy Queen on the adjacent corner. Barbecue and ice cream? Heck, that's both the food groups in one place.

We were quite hungry when we got out of the van, and the powerful scent of barbecue only made us hungrier. This place looks great — tremendous job on the decorating and the 1950s Muzak soundtrack is real barbecue eating stuff. We were happy just to be on the property.

Although there were only five of us, we filled up the dining area of The Filling Station quite well. (Our *smallest* guy is 6-foot-3, 190 pounds.) We ordered two huge combo plates and slab of ribs. As we fumbled for the cash, owner Larry Bender said, "You fellas aren't from around here, are you?" When we rattled off our hometowns, he gasped, "How in the hell did you find Lee's Summit, Missouri?"

That's when we gave G.A.S. all the credit. Larry remembered you fondly, and he clearly appreciated the significant economic impact we were about to make on his bottom line that day.

We enjoyed the ribs and chicken and sausage and turkey and pork. But we've never had beans like that.

Larry lets everything he cooks drip into the beans. Wow! It's like eating mouthfuls of sweet smoke. By far, the finest beans any of us had ever tasted.

As the meat and beans disappeared, one of us declared he wanted more. "It's not coming out of my ears yet, so I'm not full," he said. A U.S. postman came by to get lunch, so a member of our group asked for a change-of-address form. "I'm moving in and I want my wife to

forward my mail," he explained. The last of the meat slipped into our gastrointestinal tracts when Larry, who definitely can smell money through the smoke, began touting the hot fruit pies. We briefly debated whether we could eat pie and go to Dairy Queen. Larry tipped the scales when he asked if we wanted pie a la mode. (We did.)

Saturday night, after the concert (how Styx can justify not playing "Mr. Roboto" is beyond us), we again ran into the problem of no late-night barbecue availability. We cannot stress enough the importance of getting that fixed.

SUNDAY, JUNE 11

We had a Royals afternoon game and flights to catch. We desperately wanted to try L.C.'s, but it was closed. It looks tremendous from the outside, though the way a great barbecue place ought to look. We believe it's a good sign when you can't tell where the tire yard ends and the restaurant begins. Someday, when we return to Kansas City, L.C.'s will be our *second* stop.

Right after we visit Lee's Summit.

All in all, it was a successful trip to the Kansas City metropolitan area. We appreciate the ample background everyone there at G.A.S. provided, and we bless the founders of the Internet for making such research readily available. This rib's for you.

Fondest regards,

The Summit of Love gang

★ ★ ★ ★ ★ ★ ★ ★ ★ ★

G.A.S. FOR SHORT
GASTRONOMIC APPRECIATION SOCIETY

The Gastronomic Appreciation Society (G.A.S. for short) was founded in April 1997 when a bunch of guys employed at Johnson County Community College was eating lunch at Hayward's Pit Bar-B-Que and found themselves engaged in a friendly argument about which of Kansas City's barbecue joints is best. The very next month the group paid a visit to Bates City Bar-B-Q for the purpose of evaluating its fare, and thus began a series of monthly rendezvous at greasehouses throughout the metro area.

So far, the G.A.S. guys have chowed down at nearly 50 of the region's 80-plus barbecue establishments. While the purpose of these excursions is mostly fun, G.A.S takes its barbecue seriously. Some of the group's members have even been certified as official barbecue judges by the Kansas City Barbeque Society.

After each restaurant visit, unofficial G.A.S. ringleader Rick Moehring, a counselor and president of the faculty association at JCCC, posts the group's assessment of the joint on the official G.A.S. Web site **www.johnco.cc.ks.us/~rmoehrin/gas.htm.**

The Web site has inspired imitators in other cities. According to Moehring, G.A.S. "branch offices" have sprouted in Minnesota and Nebraska.

"To people who don't live in Kansas City, barbecue is seen as a form of entertainment," says Moehring. "Through our Web site we've learned that folks have actually planned vacations around visits to Kansas City and its barbecue joints."

The charter members of the Gastronomic Appreciation Society are Jeff "Sauce" Anderson, Jeffrey "It's Gotta Be Smoked, Baby" Couch, Dave "Portions" Ellis, Rick "Napkins" Moehring, Dan "Rich and Spicy" Mueller and Dick "Wanna split a pig with me?" Vallandingham. Since its inception the group has expanded to include a couple dozen other people. In 1999 the group became politically correct and began to include women in its outings.

The Gastronomic Appreciation Society's BEST OF THE BEST ★ ★ ★ Barbecue List ★ ★ ★		
	(on a scale of 1 to 10)	
Best Beans:	Fiorella's Jack Stack (Martin City)	Rating: 9.8
Best Meat:	Laura's BBQ and Stuff	Rating: 9.4
Best Ribs:	Wabash BBQ (Excelsior Springs)	Rating: 9.4
Best Fries:	LT's (since gone out of business)	Rating: 8.9
Best Sauce:	Wabash BBQ	Rating: 9.1
Best Atmosphere:	The Filling Station	Rating: 9.7
Biggest Portions:	Fiorella's Jack Stack (Martin City), Laura's BBQ and Stuff, Branding Iron	Each Rated: 9
Best Value:	K & M, The Branding Iron	Both Rated: 8.9
Best Service:	Fiorella's Jack Stack (Martin City)	Rating: 9.5
Best Overall Rating:	LC's	Rating: 9.1

NO BULL

BOARDROOM BAR B-Q

Scott O'Meara might win the prize for pitmaster least likely to succeed.

"I didn't really used to like barbecue," he says. "It all started when some ex-college roommates entered the American Royal BBQ contest back in 1983. It was just an excuse to get together."

The MU grads were hardly prodigies.

"We were fairly clueless," O'Meara admits. "We had some beer, a 20-pound prime rib and a Weber."

But there was some magic in those reunions. In three years, the group of misfits had won the American Royal contest. Catering jobs followed. Eight years later O'Meara opened Boardroom Bar-B-Q on Antioch Road.

By then, most of the other roommates had moved away and pursued their careers. O'Meara, on the other hand, was finding his former career winding down. He was working in the front office of the Kansas City Comets at the time.

"The negotiations to open the restaurant were almost complete when I learned that the Comets folded," O'Meara said. "Some people had to make tough decisions on whether to leave their job. I didn't have to make that decision. So the early slogan was 'Boardroom Bar-B-Q, an escape from the corporate bull.' "

Despite having a new baby and some unhappy in-laws, O'Meara persevered and now will match his ribs with anyone in town. But unlike most barbecue masters, he can't really thank a family heritage for his talent.

"My dad used to fire up the gas grill, which I think is sacrilege now," O'Meara says. "His idea of barbecue was getting some ribs, burn them until they were black and then cover it in sauce. That was my childhood of barbecue."

—Michael Humphrey

JOHNNY BE GOOD

JOHNNY'S BAR-B-Q

Once a year Johnny White will cook up nearly 2,000 pounds of brisket and pork butt, not a bite of which he will sell. The meat is cooked over hickory for 9 to 16 hours and then sent to the American Royal Barbecue where it will be sauced with over 400 different sauces then eaten by judges of the world's most famous barbecue sauce contest.

For the owner of Johnny's Bar-B-Q, the gesture is a tip-of-the-hat to a heritage he knows intimately.

"I got my start at Rosedale's, where my dad was the night manager," White says. "I was planning to go to Washburn to study law. But I stayed at Rosedale's and that was my education."

It has served him well. In 1977, White bought Santa Fe Trail Bar-B-Q, which he then sold in 1983 so that he could open his current establishment on Broadmoor in Johnson County.

Talking to White is like getting a graduate degree in the history of barbecue in Kansas City. He not only knows the best spots in town, but can track the genealogy of most barbecue restaurants.

"Quick's and Wyandot, for instance, they both come out of Rosedale," White says.

But White also knows the downside of the biz, which made him pause when his son Eric wanted to join him. The hours are long and can be hard.

"I have scaled back some, but I'm still working 60 hours a week," White said. "I could whine about that, but there are plenty of benefits. It's been good to me and it's been good for Kansas City," he says. "Barbecue will be here for some time."

- Michael Humphrey

Left: Johnny White and much meat.
Right: Winslow's pitmaster J.P. Clnotto pulls a brisket out of the pit.

MAXIMUM SMOKE

WINSLOW'S CITY MARKET BARBECUE

David Winslow knows restaurants. He knows them from his family, which has been a part of City Market Barbecue since 1971. And he knows them from his role as a marketing consultant for some of the hottest high-end restaurant chains in the country.

All that experience has given Winslow some insight into the secret of barbecue's success in Kansas City.

"Kansas City has been a tough place to enter for some of the better chain restaurants in this country," Winslow said. "It took me a long time to figure it out, but I realized that it's because people here like to know who's running the restaurant. They like a personality behind it."

Barbecue is nothing if not personality.

So when David's brother Don unexpectedly died in 1994, and his parents were ready to sell the restaurant, he decided to move home after 20 years away and keep the family name attached to the City Market's barbecue joint.

"It was a business decision as much as anything," Winslow said. "There were a lot of plans to renovate the City Market area at the time."

Winslow inherited a menu with deep history. The dry-rub (cooked without sauce) meat is one hallmark of the family's barbecue tradition. The "maximum smoke" pit that his brother rigged with an engineer buddy is another. Winslow's mom mastered the beans, slaw and potato salad, his brother created the wings recipe, and a former partner, John Mulvihill, created the joint's "Famous Smokie" burnt-end sandwich.

Dave says, "There's not a Winslow who goes through the door that hasn't done the cooking in this place."

—Michael Humphrey

GOIN' TO
KANSAS CITY

The Star's Sunday Magazine once asked Kathleen Purvis, food editor at The Charlotte Observer, to write about Carolina barbecue for its annual barbecue edition. She made some pretty bold and boastful claims in her article about the supposed superiority of Carolina Q. Subsequently she visited Kansas City to attend a food writers conference. Here's what Purvis had to say after partaking of genuine Cowtown barbecue.

I come before you today as a mere shell of a woman. A woman whose faith in herself has been shaken to the core.

I thought I was strong enough to do this job. I have faced whole tables of cakes at baking contests and contented myself with the thinnest of slivers. I have covered ice cream socials and taken only a single lick.

I have even judged barbecue contests. And while I know I am capable of making it through five categories with room left over for ribs, I have kept myself under control.

So why - why did I have to go to Kansas City?

Kansas City barbecue is an Olympic event. It's the melting pot of barbecue cities, the inland beach where every other barbecue style in the country washes up in a tide of smoky-sweet, tomato-based sauce. Texas brisket, North Carolina pork shoulder, Memphis ribs, all smoked over fruit woods and hickory and slapped down on white bread with lard-fried potatoes on the side.

In Kansas City, cabdrivers with Middle Eastern accents argue the fine points of Gates vs. Arthur Bryant's. The airport stocks three-packs of sauce in take-home boxes. People trash K.C. Masterpiece instead of politicians. And the supermarkets are rumored to carry more than 75 local sauces.

I have never been in a Kansas City elementary school, but I have no doubt that Kansas City kindergartners learn the ABCs as "applewood, brisket and charcoal."

When I heard that the Association of Food Journalists was holding its annual conference in Kansas City, I thought I'd better prepare myself. So I got advice from a co-worker with Kansas City roots.

He ran through the lineup of important restaurants, then summed it up. "Kansas City is barbecue and Kansas City is steak," he said. Then I swear I saw a tear in his eye. He shook his head.

"It's good living."

SET IN BONE

I tried to stick with the program. Our second day in Kansas City started with a lecture by Carolyn Wells, the co-founder of the Kansas City Barbeque Society.

"The Carolinas are the cradle of American barbecue," she said. (Smart woman, that Wells.) But Kansas City, she said, is "the epicenter of the barbecue universe."

For the rest of the day, the 85 or so writers in our group were taken to a park for a seminar on judging barbecue and a barbecue lunch with side dishes made by the Que Queens, otherwise-normal women who dress in rhinestone tiaras and compete against male barbecue teams. That's followed by lectures on smokers and barbecue sauces.

It's all very nice. But while my notes were getting that distinct odor of hickory smoke, my appetite felt like a jet that was just revving up.

And that's when I began to go astray.

A friend pulled me aside: Another writer had a rental car. She could fit three of us. Faster than you could say "slab o' ribs," we escaped and went in search of real barbecue experiences.

TAKE YOUR 'CUE

This is how you know you're in a barbecue town: When we got lost, we pulled up next to another car, rolled down the window and told the woman driving we were looking for L.C.'s, a small restaurant with a cult following.

"I want some!" she shouted, breaking into a big smile. Then she pulled in front of us and led us there through 5 o'clock traffic, even pulling over and waiting when we got caught by a red light.

L.C.'s was just as promised: no bigger than a country convenience store, and the largest thing in the place was the oven in the back, with "L" and "C" worked in metal on the doors. The napkin holders on the tables were paper towel dispensers. The sauce was peppery, the sausage — a Kansas City staple — was coarse and chunky. The fries, cut as thick as a fat man's thumb and fried in lard, were as yellow as beeswax candles.

The beef sandwich was thin-sliced meat piled several inches high among three slices of white bread that quickly dissolved, forming a cushion of sauce.

"Wonder Bread was made for barbecue," one of my companions said. I didn't say anything. My mouth was busy.

IT'S THE PITS

Brandon Billings is only 26, but he's found his niche, leading tours of barbecue restaurants for Kansas City's Convention and Visitors Bureau. Driving a van with four food writers, he assures us that Kansas City "is the second fattest city in America, after Philadelphia. But we're working on it and we're going to be first real soon."

Billings first takes us to Lil' Jake's. A diner-sized hut in a parking lot on Grand Boulevard, it's smack in the middle of downtown Kansas City. The restaurant has already closed for the day, but the owner, Danny Edwards, comes out and shows us around.

In a shed behind the tiny building, he has cookers full of meat ready to come off the fire and a stack of four cords of hickory. Real wood, downtown? Doesn't the city have a problem with the smoke?

Edwards laughs. The city is smart, he says (everybody knows enough to be happy about Kansas City's reputation.

Back in the van, we race back to the 18th and Vine district and the real Arthur Bryant's, on Brooklyn Street. Declared "the best damn restaurant in the world" by writer Calvin Trillin (a KC native, of course), Bryant's is a simple brick building with a red sign, a screen door at the front, a counter at the back and plain tables in between.

It's 3:40 on a Friday afternoon, but there are always people in line.

Counter service is fast: I order the famous open-face, burnt-ends sandwich, which is shorthand for "a bunch of meat and sauce piled on white bread." The counterman slaps down four slices of bread on butcher paper as fast as dealing a hand of cards, ladles on meat chopped up in sauce, lifts the whole thing into a plastic basket, piles on long, skinny fries and shoves it down the counter.

Arthur Bryant's sauce has its detractors.

In a straight sauce tasting, it seems gritty and overly salty with a strong taste of celery salt. But mixed with meat, particularly the popular burnt ends — the crusty outer edges of brisket - it's just right. It's like the barbe-

cue version of American-style spaghetti and meatballs: lots of sauce, little chunks of meat and the bread to pull it all together.

That left us with one taste test to go: Gates.

It would be easy to dismiss Gates as the fast food of barbecue. There are six restaurants around town, and they're all clean and efficient, with none of Arthur Bryant's funk. But that's not fair. Most people admit they prefer Gates' sauce, which is redder, smoother and smokier. And the meat on our mixed plate of ribs, brisket and ham is reliable and good, with a light touch of smoke. It's just like my Kansas City friend in Charlotte had told

me. Bryant's isn't better. It's just different.

So there I was, with a hotel room full of bottles of barbecue sauce and a notebook splattered with grease. And the awful knowledge that when I'm faced with a town full of barbecue restaurants, I have no restraint at all.

I love Carolina barbecue. But I would throw it over in a heartbeat for a chance to do Kansas City again.

That's a terrible thing to learn about yourself.

—Kathleen Purvis
The Charlotte Observer

BARBECUE
AND RACE

In 1619 a Dutch privateer arrived at Jamestown, Virginia, with a shameful cargo of captive Africans, 1,500 of which he sold to the struggling colonists — whose lives almost immediately took a turn for the better. The forced labor of these slaves had a dramatic and positive impact on the economy of the Jamestown enterprise. In truth, for the next 250 years America's economy was subsidized by the unimaginably cruel and ruthless enslavement of people kidnapped from their homes on the African continent and sold in the United States like livestock.

It wasn't the worst of the work they were forced to do, but among the tasks African slaves were compelled to perform was digging trenches, butchering animals, chopping wood, making grates, tending fires for hours on end, and serving food — bowing and scraping all the while — all so that white slaveholders could entertain their friends and neighbors with elaborate barbecues.

As documented in previous chapters of this book, virtually every reference to barbecue found in America's early historical record includes mention of the slaves who actually made the barbecue.

First person accounts written by former slaveholders years after the Civil War reflect, at best, the patronizing attitude characteristic of whites at the time and, at worst, their indifference toward the degradation inherent in slavery. Typical of these accounts are the following:

July 4th, 1859. This is Father's day to give the annual barbecue to all the Bradford black folks — all come from Live Oak Plantation, too. They number several hundred all told and vast preparation has to be made. We do not go to the barbecue for Father says we would spoil their pleasure. No white folks must go, they must feel free to enjoy themselves in their own way, but early this morning Father took me to see the pits, which were ready for the meat to be barbecued. It was a wonderful sight. Ever so many deep pits had been dug and all night fires had been burning in these pits, fires made of oakwood (for pine would spoil the taste). Over these pits of glowing coals green hickory saplings had been placed

Wedding Bells [female slave's name] and the cooks for the day were busily engaged in putting into the pits whole beeves, many of them; whole hogs, I dare not say how many. It takes a lot to feed so many strong, healthy appetites.

—From *Through Some Eventful Years*
by Susan (Bradford) Eppes (1926)

For two days and nights in advance, processions with fife and drum and bands, cannon and cavalry, had held rival parades. The fires of a great barbecue, with its long lines of parallel trenches in which under the unbroken vigilance of expert Negro cooks, whole beeves and sheep and hogs and innumerable turkeys were roasting, sent forth a savor that would have tempted the dainty palate of an Epicurus.

—From *The Old South, a Monograph*
by Howard Melancthon Hamill (1904)

★ ★ ★ ★ ★

As a result of having relied entirely on slaves to prepare barbecue, whites remained ignorant of its mysteries for nearly a half-century after Emancipation. Even after America's slaves were freed, blacks were employed by whites in the South for help in staging barbecues, since it was widely understood that only blacks knew how to barbecue.

In his 1997 book *The Confederate Housewife*, John Hammond Moore describes the attitude of most whites regarding the process of creating barbecue:

"Most [barbecues] seem to have been mass feedings held to celebrate a holiday, lure voters to a political rally or — in the 1830s and 1840s — to promote railroad construction. As such, they were of little concern to housewives. Slaves did the cooking; and, as with sliced cucumbers and garden salads, there was little reason to record a recipe, if indeed any existed. The entire process probably was viewed as an essentially male and somewhat primitive exercise unworthy of female attention."

★ ★ ★ ★ ★

Barbecuing knowledge and skills were thus passed on by African-Americans, one generation to the next, eventually becoming an economic asset almost exclusive to the black community.

At the turn of the century, enterprising African-Americans began to open the country's first legitimate commercial barbecue establishments. One of these was Henry Perry's restaurant in Kansas City.

Until the 1930s, here and elsewhere, almost all barbecue joints were owned and operated by blacks. The clientele at these restaurants, however, was frequently both black and white, even if not exactly integrated.

In *The Call's* article about Henry Perry, Mr. Perry expressed his pride at serving a loyal base of white customers.

However, while black-owned restaurants were allowed to serve white customers, as white-owned barbecue joints became more common in the 1920s and '30s, it was clear that, at these establishments, blacks were not welcome.

In the late '50s, things finally began to change. In an interview with Lolis Eric Elie for his 1996 book, *Smokestack Lightning*, Anthony Rieke, founder of Rosedale Bar-B-Q, described an incident at his restaurant that was no doubt repeated at white-owned barbecue joints across the South and Midwest:

"For years we'd serve the black people, but they'd have to take it with 'em...Well, one time, a man was coming in here, oh, every day or two and eating all the time, and a black man come and sit down beside him and we started to serving the black man. And this man that was coming in every day, he said 'You serve him, you just as well forget mine,' and he walked out. We never seen him since. That was when things was changing like that."

★ ★ ★ ★ ★

Two white barbecue joints in particular, Ollie's Barbecue in Birmingham, Alabama, and Maurice's Piggy Park in Columbia, South Carolina, became infamous for resisting desegregation with extended and nasty legal battles.

After integration began to reshape American society, traditionally all-black business districts had to compete for customers with white businesses as these gradually began to serve African-Americans.

That, says Ollie Gates, "is when you knew whether you had a good product or not. It was one thing to sell to African-Americans when they had no choice as to where they shopped or ate. But if you could keep your customers even after they could go across town to the white business, well, then you knew for sure that you had something. You had a good product."

These days, at least in Kansas City, virtually all barbecue restaurants — black-owned *and* white-owned — serve a remarkably diverse clientele. A casual observer might even hazard to say that Kansas City's barbecue joints are the most racially open and mixed dining establishments in town. Not only is it commonplace for blacks and whites to frequent the same places, it is not at all uncommon for people of African descent and people of European descent to enjoy one another's company at the same table.

Barbecue, like jazz, is uniquely American cultural expression that was first primarily perpetuated and perfected by black Americans. And like jazz, barbecue has been largely absorbed and assimilated by white Americans.

Of the 80 or so barbecue restaurants in the greater Kansas City metropolitan area, most are white-owned. Of the 10,000 or so active participants in the national barbecue competition circuit, most are white.

Gary Wells, president of the Kansas City Barbeque Society, says that his organization is doing all it can think of to encourage black teams and black individuals to compete in the barbecue contests sanctioned by the KCBS. "We really want to see more African-American involvement. That's what barbecue is all about. Welcoming everybody. Making friends. Breaking bread with your neighbors."★

CHAPTER THREE

THE BARBECUE LIFE

Major league sports organizations like identifying themselves by their initials. There's MLB, the NBA, the PGA, the NFL and the NHL, and don't forget NASCAR.

Then there's KCBS.

Operating from a miniature insurance office in south Kansas City is the world's largest organization of barbecue enthusiasts, with more than 2,500 members from all 50 states, Canada and Europe. It's the Kansas City Barbeque Society.

Founded over drinks in 1985 by Gary and Carolyn Wells and their pal Rick Welch, KCBS is now the leading contest sanctioning body for the rapidly growing sport of competitive barbecue.

Yes, folks, barbecue's a sport.

Carolyn Wells, who now serves as executive director of KCBS, estimates that in 1993 there were 100 or so barbecue contests held nationwide. In 2001 there will be about 500. KCBS sanctions almost 100 of those events, providing consistent and credible rules and a reliable judging structure. Wells says that there are over 10,000 people currently involved in competitive barbecue.

Wells and the officers and volunteers that serve on the organization's board and committees understand, however, that people take their barbecue very seriously, especially when they've been up all night cooking it, and they have a lot more fun if the contests they enter are fair.

To that end, KCBS provides uniform rules and judging criteria for contest organizers and trains contest judges. So far KCBS has trained and certified over 2,500 barbecue judges throughout the country.

The competitive barbecue season, which runs virtually every weekend from April to October, includes competitions across the United States with over $4 million in prize money awarded to winners. Purses are increasing in size each year. Some contests offer total prizes up to $40,000.

Of course, most competitors will never win a dime. Most, in fact, will spend close to $1,000 per contest on meat, fuel, seasonings, supplies, equipment, fees, and travel expenses (not the least of which are the RVs they sleep in and the rigs they need to tow their customized smokers.)

"It's unbelievable how it's grown," says KCBS co-founder Rick Welch, who lives in Parkville. "It started with a bunch of backyard cookers, and now it's international."

"We think of our group as a little off-center," Wells laughs. "We're dedicated to promoting barbecue and having fun while doing so. We barbecuers are a sort of subculture. Instead of going fishing, we barbecue. Instead of playing golf, we barbecue."

One of the society's primary means of communicating with barbecue enthusiasts around the world is its monthly 24-page plus tabloid, the "Bullsheet," which includes news of barbecue from correspondents, recipes, technique tips, contest updates and even a column on barbecue Zen.

One of KCBS's main functions is to provide technical advice to barbecue cookers. Each month over 1,000 people call the organization's offices seeking recipes, instructions and emergency cooking help.

Gary Wells, who is president of the KCBS board, once spent several hours on the phone with a woman from Canada who needed step-by-step assistance in smoking a brisket. "She called me probably every hour for eight hours so I could tell her what to do," he recalls.

"We try to act as a clearinghouse for barbecue information," Carolyn Wells says. "We get every question conceivable, from how to package a sauce and get a UPC (grocery store bar) code to how to cook a whole pig in the ground. I'm pretty sure every kook in the world has our phone number!"

★ ★ ★ ★ ★

CAROLYN WELLS

QUEEN WITH A CAPITAL QUE

Carolyn Wells isn't just the most important woman in the barbecue universe; she's the most important person in the barbecue universe.

In her role as executive director of the Kansas City Barbeque Society, Wells is to barbecue what Billy Graham is to the gospel: its most fervent evangelist.

Wells grew up in Nashville. Her grandfather was a country doctor who visited his patients on horseback until 1947 when he bought his first car. His patients were poor rural folk who often couldn't pay in cash, but Wells remembers they always somehow found a way to pay.

"Maybe they trade some service or in produce or livestock," Wells recalls. "There was a black family who every year, as part of their payment, would give my grandfather a baby goat. And they would come to the house and barbecue it for us. It was something we always looked forward to."

In the 1970s Carolyn and Gary won several barbecue cook-offs and began to earn a reputation as experts in the field.

In 1985 Carolyn was working for Wicker Barbecue Products Co. and was talking about her job with her husband, Gary Wells, and their friend Rick Welch over cocktails one night. Carolyn

mentioned that she had been fielding phone calls from local cooking teams who were interested in finding out where and when upcoming cook-offs were scheduled. This got the trio to thinking that maybe a club for barbecue cookers might be a good idea.

It was.

"I guess this was my destiny," laughs Carolyn. "I have to tell you, the relationships we've made through barbecue have been the best of my life. These are the greatest people in the world. People compete against each other for two days, but then they're clapping for whomever won. There's an amazing camaraderie in this sport.

"This is much more than just competition. It's spirit, good food, sharing. It's kind of different, but barbecue cookers are good people and Gary and I have formed some lifelong friendships."

Fulfilling her destiny hasn't always been easy, however. Being executive director of KCBS has been a "vow of poverty" Wells says. "This isn't something you do for money. This is something you do because you love it."

One of the upsides is that she gets to travel to KCBS-sanctioned contests around the country. One of the downsides is she then has to stay up all night with the contest organizers and cookers to help keep things running smoothly.

"At the end of a contest I'm really tired of barbecue," she admits. "And I'm really tired of it at the end of the season. I just want to burn my clothes, take a shower for about four days. And if I'm hungry at all, I eat a salad or maybe some ice cream. Not barbecue."

Recently, Wells has been spreading the gospel of Kansas City barbecue abroad. In 2000 she was

invited to give a seminar on the fine points of barbecue to a symposium in Italy sponsored by Slow Food International.

"The slow food movement is an effort to preserve and protect local food traditions against the threat of globalization and the encroachment of the fast food mentality," Wells explains. "(The movement) has grown tremendously over the last few years. Of course, barbecue fits right in. Barbecue is the slowest food there is."

The invite to Italy was something of a triumph for Wells, who says that in the circles of the culinary elite, barbecue is frequently seen as an "ugly step child."

"Barbecue is real," she says. "I've spent the better part of my life devoted to it. It's a treasured part of our American heritage. And now people around the world want to know what it's all about."

ARDIE DAVIS

SAUCE BOSS

Ardie Davis is a gentle man. When you meet him, you are first impressed by his amiable smile and next by his sincerity and graciousness. If you exchange personal histories you'll soon learn that he was a conscientious objector during the Vietnam War. And no matter how many barbecue stories he tells you, and he's got plenty of 'em, you suspect that deep inside his brisket-eating soul is a vegetarian plotting, non-violently of course, to get out.

But Ardie Davis' inner vegetarian will have to wait a long time to emerge. This guy loves barbecue too much to forsake his carnivorous ways anytime soon.

"I love it because it appeals to the things that matter most to me," he says. "Barbecue is a 'bridge food' spanning the gap between different races and classes. If you can enjoy food together, barriers drop. Barbecue helps me relate to my working-class roots. It hits you in primal places."

That, and it tastes good.

In the summer of 1984, Ardie Davis was enjoying one of those rare weekends husbands and fathers seldom get. Wife Gretchen and the kids were away in Minnesota. Ardie had a Ry Cooder album cranked up on the stereo while he relaxed with a book; Roadfood by Jane and Michael Stern.

"They listed over 80 barbecue restaurants in their book," Ardie recalls. "I thought, 'I'm never going to be able to visit all those restaurants.' So I started writing them and asking for their sauce."

Soon he'd acquired quite a collection of sauces and that's when the idea hit him for a barbecue sauce contest.

On October 6, 1984, Ardie and Gretchen and about 70 of their closest friends gathered on the

Davises' porch for the first "Diddy-Wa-Diddy Barbecue Sauce Contest" (named after the Ry Cooder song playing at the moment of Davis' inspiration). They took an oath to preserve "truth, justice, excellence in barbecue and the American way of life" and proceeded to pass judgment on 104 different sauces.

After that things quickly got out of hand.

The contest proved to be such a novel and popular idea that it took on a life of its own. Word spread faster than a grease fire in a Weber kettle, and by 1987 the contest had grown so large Ardie negotiated a handoff to the American Royal Barbecue and the event was renamed the American Royal International Barbecue Sauce, Rub & Baste Contest.

Now there are more than 400 sauces entered in the annual competition, including several from foreign countries. It's the largest sauce contest in the world.

"People put a lot of ego into their sauces," Davis says, "so when I'm writing about them I was always mindful that it is precious stuff to the people who make it. It's sort of 'love me, love my sauce.'

" Mindful. Precious. Love. Typical of Ardie Davis to use such words when he speaks of the relationship between people and barbecue. Typical of a gentle man.

Ardie Davis' barbecue sauce-loving alter ego is Remus Powers, a persona he created as a tribute to the stories of Brer Rabbit and a man he remembers from his childhood, a "James Dean-type" automobile mechanic Davis knew simply as "Powers."

CHIEF CHEF

PAUL KIRK

★ ★ ★ ★ ★ ★ ★ ★ ★ ★ ★

Paul Kirk's contribution to barbecue is roughly equivalent to the contribution of Vince Lombardi to football and Jack Nicklaus to golf. Combined. Except in Paul Kirk's case he's alive and in his prime.

Paul Kirk is the world's greatest barbecue cooker *and* the world's greatest barbecue coach. These are titles he'd never claim for himself. But then, if you asked him about it he wouldn't exactly deny it.

He knows he's good at what he does, and he's got the credentials to prove it. He's won more than 400 cooking and barbecue awards, including seven world championships, the American Royal Open and the Jack Daniel's Invitational. And he's not done yet.

Paul Kirk's father was a TWA pilot who, when he was home, would sometimes build a barbecue pit in the backyard from cinderblocks and iron grates and then cook up some ribs and some chickens for family or friends. This is Kirk's earliest memory of barbecue and it still flavors his feelings about it.

"Barbecue is all about hospitality," he says. "Barbecue brings family and friends together. And it makes family and friends out of strangers. Anybody and everybody is welcome at a barbecue."

Kirk's mother was a good cook and got him interested in things culinary.

"I put myself through college at St. Mary's of the Plains in Dodge City by cooking in restaurants," he says. "I took some classes at the Johnson County Community College, but mostly I'm self-taught. I just love to cook. I guess I have a God-given talent, and I've tried to put it to good use."

Kirk has put his talent to good use most of his adult life as a professional chef. And for much of that time he's been a dominant fixture on the competitive barbecue circuit.

In 1981, Kirk was working at a restaurant that had its own barbecue pit.

"I was doing all the cooking using my own sauces and herbs," he recalls. "The owner convinced me I had a special touch with barbecue and kept urging me to enter the American Royal contest. I did, and won first place with my chicken and second with my barbecued ribs. I've been competing ever since."

While barbecue has been a passion for Kirk for over two decades, teaching has increasingly become the primary focus of his professional life.

"I used to enter at least 15 contests or more a year," he says. "But I've been cutting back to concentrate on teaching. Cooking barbecue is a hobby, but I'm very serious about teaching. My goal is to promote Kansas City barbecue."

Kirk has trained professional chefs and taught classes for the general public across the United States. He's observed that the most common mistake backyard chefs make is that they're impatient.

"They're in too much of a hurry," he says. "They don't control the fire, don't take time to learn the fundamentals and don't really work at it. Your equipment doesn't make any difference if you don't control the fire. I have a rig worth $8,000 that I can cook 150 slabs of ribs on at a time, but you can do just as well on a cheap grill — if you control the fire.

"The secret of success is being conscientious. And frankly, you need to have fun. You have to enjoy what you're doing, if you're going to do it right."

And if you're going to do it right, learn to do it from Paul Kirk. Because there's probably nobody who knows how to do it better.

"Barbecue just gets bigger every year," he points out. "People live this. It's a lifestyle. It's not a whim or a passing fad.

"When people ask me, 'How can you justify paying $300 to $500 a pop for a cooker?' I say, 'Didn't you pay $15,000 for a used bass boat last year? Don't you go to the lake and burn up $200 in gas pulling those kids around on skis?'

"I say, 'You know what? At least I get to eat every weekend.' "

THE AMERICAN ROYAL BARBECUE

THE WOODSTOCK OF BARBECUE

I t's a what-came-first-the-chicken-or-the-egg kind of question. Is barbecuing really just a good excuse to have a party, or is having a party a good excuse to barbecue?

Who cares? Gimme a beer and pass the ribs.

The American Royal Barbecue — The World Series Of Barbecue Contests — is the Cowtown's best and biggest party.

The barbecue itself is to the American Royal Barbecue what the birthday is to a birthday party. It is the reason for the party. But after the song, the cake and the presents, well, then it's party time, and the birthday part of the equation becomes secondary to the party part. After the smoke clears and the judges have declared the winners, barbecue ceases to be the object of the American Royal Barbecue contest.

It becomes dinner.

And the Kemper Arena parking lot becomes Party City.

On a Friday afternoon, smack in the middle of the event, sweet blue smoke rises from hundreds of cookers as briskets, ribs, pork butts and sausages are gently and slowly transformed into barbecue by burning apple wood, cherry, hickory and oak. The Invitational competition is over. The 65 elite teams in the Invitational - champions all - are anxiously awaiting the results of the judging. Tomorrow is the judging in the Open competition.

And tonight... Tonight is the party. The party. There will be music, dancing and libation. Already musicians are unpacking their instruments, speakers and microphones. Volunteers are setting up tables and chairs. And in between tending the fires and mopping the meat, the cooks are preparing vast quantities of beans, potato salad and coleslaw. The libation has been under way for quite a while. Messrs. Jim Beam and Jack Daniel are in attendance.

Tonight the West Bottoms will be jammed with carloads of Cowtowners reveling in an honest-to-goodness Kansas City tradition. This will be a world-class party.

The American Royal is "the Academy Awards of barbecue," according to *The New York Times Magazine.*

"Cowtown" cartoonist Charlie Podrebarac calls it "the Woodstock of barbecue."

According to Carolyn Wells, executive director of the Kansas City Barbeque Society, the American Royal competition is the "World Series of barbecue, the Super Bowl of barbecue and the ultimate backyard barbecue."

To the teams participating in the event, the American Royal is the toughest, most prestigious competition on the barbecue contest circuit.

As measured by the number of people attending, the barbecue at the Memphis in May festival, on the banks of the Mississippi, is bigger than the Royal. It is also, according to Wells, quite a bit rowdier. "I call it the 'Three-Day Toot on the River,' " she says. "The Royal is much more family-friendly. Just as you would expect in Kansas City."

Another of the major contests is held at the annual Houston Livestock Show and Rodeo. Wells says the Houston event is dominated by large corporate cooking teams. "It has its own atmosphere," she says. "It's much more formal and businesslike. You come back to Kansas City and appreciate what we do here so much more. We really do know how to party. In a good way."

★ ★ ★ ★ ★ ★ ★ ★ ★ ★

Yₒu can't be a writer about food at The Kansas City Star and not eventually write about the American Royal Barbecue. It's not only one of the most important culinary and cultural events in Kansas City, it's one of the most important food events in the nation. Here are some fine stories from some of The Star's best writers that capture some of what the American Royal Barbecue is all about. The first two, by arts and entertainment writer Brian McTavish and former Star restaurant critic John Martellaro, form a tribute to one of Kansas City's finest competitive barbecue teams (Three Little Pigs). The third piece is from our current food editor, Jill Wenholdt Silva. The last story is by features writer Karen Uhlenhuth.

—D.W.

TALES FROM THE PIT...

Chicken Larry Marks has a few tricks up his smoker for the American Royal Barbecue Contest.

Not that the 62-year-old Hallmark Cards retiree will discuss them freely with anyone but the Three Little Pigs.

Marks, his wife, Joan, and son Chris are the nucleus of the Three Little Pigs competitive barbecue team. Earlier this month it was judged to be the grand champion out of 68 teams at the 11th Annual Blue Springs Barbeque Blaze Off State Championship Barbecue Contest - the longest-running barbecue battle in the four-state area next to the American Royal.

The Three Little Pigs placed fifth or better in all divisions at Blue Springs, including a blue ribbon in chicken.

Mmmm, that chicken.

"It places well," Joan Marks said during a recent strategy session at Joan and Larry's southeast Kansas City home. Parked in the driveway, like a steel-case ode to the human salivary gland, was the couple's $2,500 jet-black barbecue smoker.

But, until recently, nothing was helping the Marks' quest for a prize-winning chicken breast.

"Not mentioning any names," said Larry Marks, trying to suppress his growing grin, "but the part that was cooking the chicken was having trouble getting out of last place."

"Chicken's a tough category," Chris Marks said.

"It was me," Joan confessed, chuckling at her husband's not-so-thinly veiled chiding. "It was very hard. I was down in the basement."

Then, a few months ago at a small contest, Larry

tried cooking chicken. His bird was heating up too quickly when he simultaneously avoided disaster and stumbled on his secret "sweet-hot" chicken breast recipe...which was?

The Three Little Pigs won't tell. But they like to talk among themselves.

"We do a lot of talking about how we prepare things - how we want to change it, if we want to change it," said Chris, 33.

Larry attributes a good deal of the team's growing success to skills he honed for 34 years as a manager for Hallmark Cards.

"At Hallmark you had to work as a team," Larry said. "And this is what we've tried to do here, because any other way it wouldn't work."

This year's Three Little Pigs, including son-in-law Tim Bowman and family friend Dave Ritter, increased its weekend competitions from 10 to 13, including next month's Jack Daniel's World Championship Invitational in Lynchburg, Tenn.

And the '94 prize money has piled up: $850 at Blue Springs; $500 for being judged grand champion at the Northwest Kansas State Championship in McLouth, Kan., $575 for best brisket at the Adrian's Barbecue Sauce/George Brett Cook-off at The Woodlands race tracks, and a cool 41,000 for being judged reserve grand champ among more than 70 teams at the

★ ★ ★ ★ ★ ★ ★ ★ ★

Midwest Regional competition in Gladstone.

If that seems like a lot of cash, subtract the $150 that a team has to pay for ribs, chicken, pork, brisket, sausage and other choice cuts of meat before every contest. Then there's the typical $50 to $100 entry fee. By the end of the day, let alone the summer, just breaking even can be a thrill.

"This is the first time that we've had enough money to be even," Joan said. "Before, it's all come out of Mom and Dad's pocket."

Now looms the 15th annual American Royal Barbecue. The Three Little Pigs will compete against 300 teams in the open and invitational categories. At stake is more than $30,000 in cash and prizes. And one more thing, according to Monty Spradling, sponsorship chairman of this weekend's big event.

"It's the old ego," Spradling said. "Once you become good, you want to be very good. That's the calling and that's the addicting part."

Larry Marks' friendly obsession with barbecue began in 1990, when he and a neighborhood chum showed up with an ordinary backyard grill at a Raytown barbecue contest.

"We entertained too many people and our meat didn't get done," Larry recalled. "My friend had a beautiful looking turkey. But it walked."

"It was raw inside," Joan said

"It was hilarious," Chris said.

It was a start. The next year Larry took formal barbecuing classes and inducted Chris' help at a handful of area competitions. In '92 Joan came on board and Larry was ready to retire from Hallmark (but not from life.

"I knew that I had to get out and meet people," he said. "I'm a people person. And this was the best way of doing it."

The Marks crew knew there was no going back when Larry bought a pro-quality smoker, which slowly and flavorfully cooks meat through indirect heat generated by a burning mix of charcoal and fruit-flavored wood chips.

"I said, 'I don't want that thing sitting in my driveway,'" Joan said.

Larry told Joan it would fit in the garage.

"We only missed by about a foot," Chris said.

Larry and Chris have tried to be more precise about everything else, from carefully calculating their cooking times and temperatures to taking account of wind and weather.

A log is kept of any changes in team recipes, contest results and every known variable that may have contributed to any outcome. It all ends up in a team notebook kept up to date by Chris, a computer software engineer.

"We do good when it rains," Chris said, because the computer tells him so.

"I graph it all out," he said. "You give me numbers, I can make them work."

It's a competitive streak that didn't come from his father, Chris and his mother agree.

"I'm the one that has to calm them down," Larry said. "Our goal is just to win one ribbon per contest. We don't always achieve it, but we try. I'm one of those guys that if we win, we win. If we don't we don't."

Even so, Larry takes Chris' help slapping on ribs as early as 4 a.m. for a frenzied noon-hour competition that can upset the saucepan of the most well-prepared barbecuer. It may look like one, but it's no picnic yanking off different pieces of meat at hectic 30-minute intervals to be rigorously judged for appearance, taste and tenderness. Oh, and by the way, the taste score is doubled.

"We're yelling at each other the whole time," Joan said.

"Always," Chris said.

"It's like, 'Oh, this isn't tender enough,'" Joan said. "And they'll say, 'Well, how do you like this?' And I'll say, 'No, I like that.'"

Suddenly, someone might say, "Is Dad on one of his walk-abouts?"

"Sometimes, we won't find him for four hours," Chris said.

"When it comes time to cut the brisket, it's 'Where's Dad? Where's Dad? Go find Dad!'" Joan said.

"I had to cut it at Blue Springs," Chris said, "because we couldn't find him."

"It should," "Chicken Larry" added, "be a relaxing time."

—Brian McTavish
October 1994

★ ★ ★ ★ ★ ★ ★ ★ ★ ★

THE BIG SHOTS OF BARBECUE

Winning the Grand Championship at the American Royal Barbecue means finishing first among more than 300 competitors in a blind taste-test. Doing it even once is a feat.

The Three Little Pigs, a Blue Springs-based cooking team, have triumphed in the Royal's Open Division two years in a row. And in 1997, the group won the Royal's Invitational Division, an elite competition limited to teams that have won other major championships.

Suffice it to say, there's some serious smokin' going on here.

"The chances of that happening, the odds, are just phenomenal," said Carolyn Wells, executive director of the Kansas City Barbeque Society, which sanctions barbecue competitions across the country, including the Royal.

"It about knocked me over," said chief cook Chris Marks, 38, of Independence. His mother, Joan Marks of Blue Springs, is "pit boss" of the team founded by his late father, Larry Marks.

"We didn't place in any of the categories, so it was a shocker that we won it all."

Joan Marks, 63, said: "We're kind of stunned. But we're happy.

"Years ago, when we first started, I remember we thought, 'If we could just win one ribbon at the American Royal, we would be so happy.'"

The Grand Champion is determined by combined points from five categories: chicken, pork ribs, beef brisket, sausage and pork shoulder or butt. Wells said it was across-the-board consistency that won the day for the Three Little Pigs, a team that also includes David Ritter of Kansas City.

"What's really significant is, they got no individual ribbon but were still the top point-getter," Wells said.

We'll give you the bad news first: Despite their success - including 21 grand championships in the last seven years - the Pigs have no plans to turn pro and open a restaurant.

"It's pretty hard. If you want to open a (restaurant) business, it's so extensive. It's a lot of hours," said Chris Marks, who works as a software engineer for Integrated Corporate Solutions of Overland Park. "I like doing it for fun, and I think that would take all the fun out of it."

Now the good news: They're not shy about sharing at least some of their secrets.

Chris Marks said he buys his meat over the counter at a local market and uses a commercial dry rub seasoning he orders over the Internet from John Willingham's in Memphis, Tenn. He smokes the meat with wild cherry wood.

But they're not giving away all their secrets.

"I think our secret is our barbecue sauce, and that is made by me. It's ours," Joan Marks said. "Nobody else has a sauce that tastes like ours. Everybody is dying to find out what we use, and I'm not going to tell."

Joan Marks has been a member of the Kansas City Barbeque Society board of directors, which Wells points out is a separate entity from the Royal contest, where judges rate samples identified only by code number.

"They're a good, clean team, and they represent the barbecue community very well," Wells said. "And obviously their food tastes wonderful."

It was Larry Marks, known as "Boss Hog," who started the team.

"They started their first contest in Raytown with a tent and a little backyard cooker," Chris Marks recalled. "The next year he retired from Hallmark and we bought him an Oklahoma Joe's trailer" - a large competition smoker on wheels.

"Now we're up to a 35-foot RV and trailer smokers," Chris Marks said. "We used to cook pretty heavy on the circuit until my dad died two years ago. Then we slowed down quite a bit."

As in past years, Joan Marks cooked while wearing the team jacket the members originally had custom-made for Larry. It's black with teal and pink lettering - and, for her, a bit unwieldy.

"That's our lucky charm. It's very large. He was about 230 pounds and 6-foot-1, but it just feels comfortable on me and it makes me feel like he's helping us," Joan Marks said.

Wells said Larry Marks was a popular figure on the barbecue contest circuit.

"He was a very much beloved guy, and they're sure carrying on his legacy very well," she said.

— John Martellaro
October 1999

TRUTH, JUSTICE AND THE BBQ WAY

In a world full of Arby 'ques and McRibs, judges for the American Royal World Championship Invitational take a solemn oath to uphold "truth, justice, excellence in barbecue and the American way of life."

Wearing suspenders with pigs on them, Ron Harwell of Trinity, Ala., was among this year's crop of judges.

"This is what I do instead of play golf," he says.

Jay Fowler, Mike Lake and Charles Barnlund — all from various parts of Illinois - volunteer to judge year after year.

Bob Sloan, a New York City-based cookbook author, is judging for the first time.

And there are the usual local chefs and media people who make the trek to barbecue Mecca again and again.

"They get a good cross section of people. It doesn't matter if you're a bank president or whatever," Barnlund says, surveying the judges seated in groups of six.

For the last decade the first weekend in October has become synonymous with the American Royal World Championship Invitational Barbecue. Billed by organizers as the world's largest barbecue contest, the best cookers and eaters from across the country gather for a huge barbecue bash in the parking lot of Kemper Arena.

A RIB BY ANY OTHER NAME

Goofy team names are a part of the sport of competitive barbecue. At the 2000 American Royal Barbecue there were nearly 400 teams competing and almost all of them had really silly names. Here are some of my favorites:

Any Pork in a Storm

Beverly Grillbillies

Bite My Butt BBQ

Burn Rate

Carnivore Club

Don't Burn the Beer

Drinkers with a Bar-B-Que Problem

Fat Daddy & The Grazers

Grillas

The Last Supper

Oink, Moo, and Cock-a-doodle-doo

Pig Newton

The Pork Pimps

Skews-Me Barbecue

Slaughterhouse Five

Smokin' Elvi

Sparkle Plenty

Squeal of Approval

Team Stupid

Ziggy Piggy

—D.W.

★ ★ ★ ★ ★ ★ ★ ★ ★ ★

And for those who judge, they quite literally have a full plate.

In fact, if you sample everything that is served to you in the 2 1/2 hours of competition, you'll have eaten 2 to 3 pounds of meat!

Judges also must follow the niggling details of protocol, such as keeping your fingers clean. Not an easy task when devouring ribs, but the electronic Scantron judging sheet requires attention to details.

"It doesn't like barbecue juice or sauce, and it's not particularly happy if it's used as a napkin. It will spit it out," Kansas City Barbeque Society volunteer Lee Newlin says.

And it goes without saying that the contestants take their judging seriously. After all, they can win hefty trophies and bragging rights for years to come, so Newlin reminds the judges each contestant has invested a lot of time, money and enthusiasm to be there.

So it's no wonder that judging has become a serious art form as promoted by the Kansas City Barbecue Society, a not-for-profit organization whose members founded the Royal contest. The KCBS even offers judging seminars that teach contestants what to look for and make everyone feel they got a fair shake.

Certainly, it's wise to have a uniform set of rules to judge by. But when it comes to eating, thank goodness there's more to it than the fast-food versions so much of America is weaned on.

—Jill Wendholt Silva
October 1999

★ ★ ★ ★ ★

COOKS FUSS OVER DETAILS OF BARBECUE

Joe Davidson hurried into his tent from his big barbecue grill bearing a pan of chicken breasts. He bent over them tenderly, reverently.

"That's my centerpiece right there," he whispered, and carefully placed one of the golden globes in the middle of a bed of lettuce. "I always want to have one piece they see just as it came off the grill."

While Davidson sliced several more breasts to provide samples for the six judges who would assess his work at the American Royal Open Barbecue competition, his aide-de-camp, Jay Johnson of Stillwater, Oklahoma, carried out the parsley detail, tucking in sprigs here and there. Weighty considerations, these. Davidson wiped a daub of grease from the edge of the styrofoam box.

"It's beautiful," declared Davidson, of Seguin, Texas. "Where's the camera?"

Another member of his party stepped forward and clicked the shutter, capturing the chicken for posterity.

Then, slipping briefly out of Martha Stewart mode, Davidson and Johnson stepped toward each other, right hands raised overhead. They

★ ★ ★ ★ ★ ★ ★ ★ ★ ★

slapped them together in a high-five, then cried, "Hogamaniacs!"

It was a battle cry they would repeat four more times that afternoon as they sent their other towel-wrapped entries — ribs, pork, brisket and sausage - to the judges seated at long plastic-covered tables inside the American Royal building.

For some 370 barbecuers, Saturday afternoon was the moment of truth, when their hours and days of effort and hundreds of dollars invested would translate into prizes for a select few at the competition.

While the contestants fussed over smoked flesh, a smattering of visitors immersed themselves in the delectable smells, and smoke, of the parking lot scene. If they came expecting to partake, however, they were disappointed.

"The public really hates that," said John Ross, a member of the Kansas City Barbeque Society who orchestrated the judging. "They pay an entry fee of $8 and find out they can't get any barbecue. We'd like to make 'em happy, but it's not up to us."

The Kansas City health code prohibits passing out samples, he said.

At a small food court, visitors with a hankering for barbecue could choose from fried onions or potatoes, gelato or frozen custard, burgers and sausages and funnel cakes. But barbecue? It was not for sale.

It wasn't the easiest of barbecuing weekends. The weather, damp and cold late Friday night and into Saturday, played havoc with the temperature of the grills, many of them large enough to merit their own trailers.

Tom Stoner, a contestant also known as Chief Cooker from Shannon, Ill., had slept no more than three hours between Wednesday, when he arrived and began stoking his fire, and Saturday afternoon, when the process was reaching a fever pitch.

Aided by a couple of friends and competitors, Stoner pulled five slabs of ribs off his little Weber grill — his barbecue on wheels had lost too much heat overnight to be salvaged.

"We're trying to decide which is the best rack," said his friend Jack Fosdick, a fellow barbecuer.

The group settled on the winning rack, painted the top with a little sauce, then tried to wipe off an errant drop that had dribbled onto the exposed face of one rib.

No detail too small.

—Karen Uhlenhuth
October 1999

Chris Marks of the Three Little Pigs barbecue team takes a good whiff of his cooking before judging at the 2000 American Royal Barbecue.

★ ★ ★ ★ ★ ★ ★ ★ ★ ★

FIREFIGHTER LOVES SMOKE

Jim Fussell, *The Star's* barbecue writer par excellence, wrote this entertaining piece in October 1997 as that year's American Royal Barbecue got underway.

—D.W.

Mark Bishop strode slowly into the KCFX-FM studios, a man on a mission. In his arms he cradled two steaming racks of ribs in a white plastic bag that was powerless against the seductive smell. Gently, he set the food on a counter and smiled at midday host Lauren Holladay, who shot him a knowing grin in return.

"I can eat barbecue like nobody's business," Holladay said, sitting cross-legged in a small studio as she spun classic rock tunes.

"I brought you some barbecue ribs from KC Masterpiece."

"You are a doll!" she gushed, eyeing the package like a lion eyes a limping gazelle.

Ahh, lunchtime largess!

Mark Bishop had struck again!

Officially the 37-year-old Bishop is a Kansas City, Kan., firefighter. But this week he wasn't fighting fires as much as he was lighting them.

You see, Bishop is a barbecue ambassador for the American Royal Barbecue, and his role is to get people excited about the two-day competition that starts today in the parking lot of the American Royal. This year's event will feature hundreds of contestants from around the world. Bishop is trying to spread the word. His strategy?

Barbecue bribery, pure and simple.

But let him explain.

"All I do is get on the telephone and call the television and radio stations and say, 'I'll bring you some barbecue if you put me on the air for five or 10 minutes to promote the American Royal Barbecue Contest,'" he said. "And usually there is no hesitation - it's like 'when do you want to be here?' They all love it!" And why not?

It's smoky and sweet, not stuck-up or snooty. It's genuine bona-fide barbecue booty!

"I'm going to talk a lot about you on the air," Holladay said.

"Cool," Bishop said.

Chalk up another one for the baron of barbecue publicity.

Tracy Satterfield, barbecue coordinator for the American Royal Barbecue, praised Bishop for his volunteer efforts.

"Mark Bishop has been a gift from heaven for the American Royal Barbecue," she said. "He spends hours and hours every year getting publicity for us. We are very lucky to have him."

Bishop got involved with the American Royal Barbecue about five years ago.

"My brother-in-law's (relatives) were doing the volunteer work at the food court at the American Royal," he said. "So one year he says, 'Hey, you ought to come down and we ought to try to help out a little bit.'"

Bishop stayed the whole day and came back the next. Now he's on the public relations committee and volunteers to cook meat, which is paid for by the American Royal Barbecue. Today he is one of several barbecue backers who try to exchange eats for exposure.

Back at KCFX, Bishop makes small talk as Holladay plays another song - "Won't Get Fooled Again" by the Who. By this time the smell of barbecue has permeated the room and Holladay is beaming, promising publicity before Bishop even asks.

There would be no on-air interview like he had earlier that morning on KSHB, Channel 41, though. Holladay's boss was out, she explained, and she'd couldn't do an actual interview without proper authorization.

"But this is a big event, and I appreciate this," she reassured Bishop. "We will hit this several times. And I will leave it for other personalities, too."

Bishop quickly laid the groundwork for an even greater promotion next year.

"What I'd like to do next year is get a Lauren Live at Lunch down there," he said. "That would be fun, she said. "Barbecue heaven!"

In addition to bringing barbecue from KC Masterpiece, a major

American Royal Barbecue sponsor, Bishop also smokes his own barbecue meat — including ribs, pork roasts and brisket - to give away.

Last weekend was no exception.

Slowly he opened the doors of the 4,000-pound, 4-foot-long "Dragon" smoker in the back of KCK fire station No. 3. When he did, the mouthwatering smell of more than $200 worth of slow roasted ribs, roasts and beef brisket poured hot and sweet into the grateful air.

"I'm going to go ahead and take the temperature and see what's going on," he said. "It's at 140 degrees. She's cooking nice. Really nice. It's only been on for four hours. Four more to go."

He sprayed a golden liquid on the meat.

"Apple juice," he said. "Puts on a little glaze. About every 20 minutes I squirt 'em down. Then a little bit later I change it and I add a few things to it that I can't tell you about because it's top secret. There are a lot of secrets to barbecuing. When you get down there to the Royal, guys won't tell you nothin'."

Has he ever entered the contest?

"No," he said. "Too busy doing everything else."

Like taking barbecue to television and radio stations. Next on his agenda: KBEQ-FM and WDAF, Channel 4, among others.

But on this day, he aimed his good-natured barbecue bribery at KCFX. And he succeeded. Then it was time to go.

Holladay flashed a wide smile and called one last farewell as Bishop left the barbecue and stepped into the hall.

"Dig in," he said.

"Oh yeah," she called back, as the Who's "Won't Get Fooled Again" approached it's explosive conclusion. "I'm going to be up to my elbows in barbecue, baby!"

And just how did that make her feel?

Let's just say Roger Daltry said it all for her.

"YEAAAAAAAAA!" The Who's frontman exploded in the song's transcendent rebel yell.

Exactly.

—Jim Fussell

☆ ☆ ☆ ☆ ☆ ☆ ☆ ☆ ☆

CHARLIE
PODREBARAC

In the way that a politician knows he matters when cartoonist Garry Trudeau lampoons him in "Doonesbury," one of the ways we know how much barbecue matters in Kansas City is how often it shows up in Charlie Podrebarac's "Cowtown."

It shows up a lot.

Podrebarac's single-panel cartoon has provided comic relief to readers of *The Kansas City Star's Sunday Star Magazine* since 1986. "Cowtown" is populated by clueless losers who can't get a date; Elvis and his imitators; self-absorbed, black-clad, espresso-swilling hipsters; self-absorbed, cell-phone addicted, cocktail-swilling yuppies; enough clowns to fit into a circus car; and farm animals that talk.

And guys in their backyards ruining briskets in their Webers, and guys out at Arrowhead hogging five parking spaces with semi-truck-sized smokers.

By celebrating and poking fun at Kansas City's barbecue culture, "Cowtown" has helped keep it healthy and fixed firmly in our collective imagination.

Podrebarac grew up on Strawberry Hill in Kansas City, Kansas, and lives now in Westwood.

Though Charlie's been more successful than most professional cartoonists, inasmuch as he's actually been able to make a living at it, there's no doubt he could have achieved greater success if he'd moved to New York or Los Angeles. But, so far, he's content to stay put.

"I love Kansas City," Podrebarac confesses. "Besides me, I think the biggest boosters for our city are the people moving here from other regions of the coun-

try. We hook with barbecue, and they stay because Kansas City is a great place to grow roots."

Perhaps it was inevitable, but Podrebarac has recently crossed over and is now no longer simply a wry observer of Kansas City's barbecue scene. He's a part of it. Podrebarac and wife Alicia have partnered with Jeff and Joy Stehney of Oklahoma Joe's to produce and market a line of barbecue sauces, the labels of which feature images from "Cowtown."

"Diving into the sauce business in *this* town seems like a dubious quest," Podrebarac admits. "But when your partners - i.e., the people with the recipes - are multiple award-winning contest winners and successful restaurateurs, the endeavor is actually fun and an interesting challenge."

Maybe the main reason Podrebarac has stayed in Kansas City in spite of opportunities to leave is that it's such a rich source of material for his cartoons. "Barbecue in Kansas City is out of control," he observes. "We barbecue year-round. We've formed clubs, teams, even a *society*. We build exotic Rube Goldberg-like iron cookers. Every year the contests get bigger and better and new joints keep opening. Our citizens discuss the nuances of various woods, meat, sauces and rubs everywhere, from cocktail parties to church.

"Something should be done to stop this madness, before it really gets out of hand. But not by me."

Clockwise from top left: Tim McCracken (left) and Tim Kliethermes with their pink 1953 Chevy pick-up smoker; The Lipton barbecue team (from left), Ron Storey, Bill Mansell and Kevin Schwede; The "Swine Flew" barbecue team (from left), Cam Morrison, Marty Edwards, Terrence Crane, Timothy Hanssen and Bill Rousseau; Ed "Fast Eddy" Maurin and his happy pig. Center: Shawn Foltz checks on the Q in the Camcorn team cooker.

THE GRAND BARBECUE **77**
THE BARBECUE LIFE

THE GREAT LENEXA
BARBEQUE BATTLE
KANSAS STATE CHAMPIONSHIP

The Kansas City area is home to two of the top four barbecue contests in the world: the American Royal Barbecue and the Great Lenexa Barbeque Battle Kansas State Championship.

That's like having Wimbledon and the U.S. Open tennis tournaments in the same city every year. If that were the case, wouldn't you say that city has a right to call itself the Tennis Capital of the World? Of course you would. And if one city was host to both the Masters and PGA Championship golf tournaments wouldn't it be logical to call that city the Golf Capital of the World? Of course it would.

So all you other cities out there with your lame claims to be barbecue capitals, you can forget about it. Hosting the American Royal Barbecue - the World Series and Academy Awards of barbecue - would be reason enough for you all to just give Kansas City the barbecue capitalship and go home. But the fact that we are also home to the Great Lenexa Barbecue Battle/Kansas State Championship - the Rose Bowl and Emmy Awards of barbecue - well, that just cinches it.

They call it a "battle." And the competitors are intense in their desire for victory. But, as you'll see in these 1997 vignettes by former *Star* reporter Susan White, the Great Lenexa Barbecue Battle represents a unique form of warfare. Its whimsical and warm. Call it *friendly fire*.

Ted and Donna McClure Grand Champions of the 1997 Great Lenexa Barbeque Battle.

Brian A. McNichols really didn't want to miss the chance to compete in the 1997 Great Lenexa Barbecue Battle.

In fact, he flew in from Pittsburgh, from a three-month business assignment, just in time to set up camp at Sar-Ko-Par Trails Park, site of the competition. His team, "Green Apple Trot," also includes Kip Nichols, his son-in-law, and Brian Scott McNichols, his son

and team leader.

"I can't wait," said the elder McNichols. "I plan on staying the night at the barbecue, but we'll take it one hour at a time. I am sure the guys will have everything in order and ready to start." The team's name comes from the green apple wood used in the smokers and the green apple glaze used on pork.

★★★★★

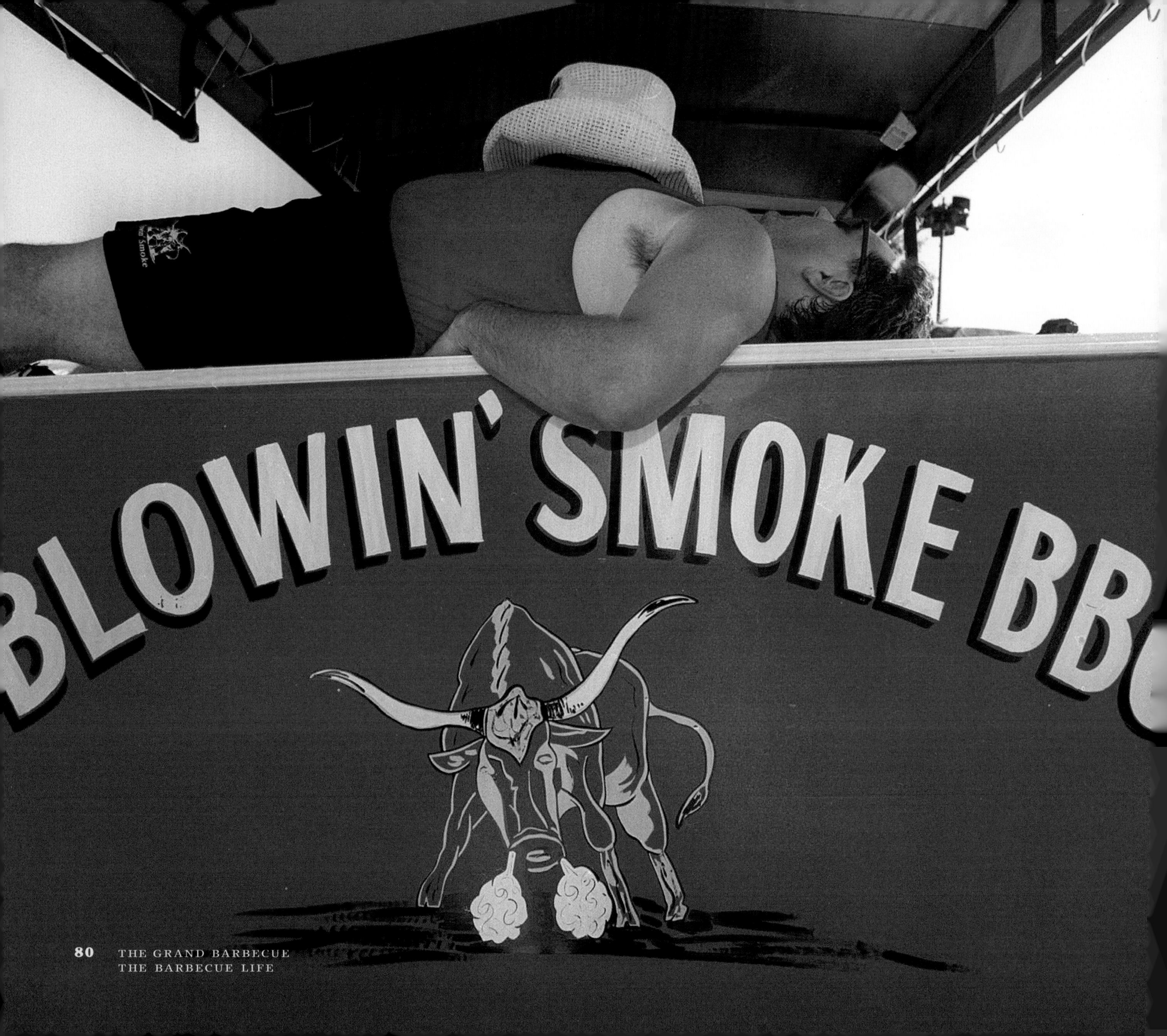
BLOWIN' SMOKE BB

★ ★ ★ ★ ★ ★ ★ ★ ★ ★

Most teams will set up as early as Friday morning, and others start setting up Friday afternoon around Rose's Pond in the park. Some teams with bigger vehicles will set up Thursday so they have more "elbow room" to move around, said Lenexa Parks and Recreation Director Bill Nicks.

Each year, teams from all over the United States vie for the grand champion title, cash prize, an Oklahoma Joe's Smoker and the champion's banner.

"When the winning team gets that banner they *will* cry," Nicks said. "You've been up all night and cooking all day."

By comparison, the first event in 1982 had 12 teams, 12 judges and a few hundred visitors. The grand prize was a case of bottled beer, from which one bottle was missing.

The barbecue battle has been a McNichols family tradition since Brian A. McNichols first competed on the "Dung-Ho" team in the early years of the contest. In recent years the younger McNichols also has worked the contest as a city staff member.

Brian Scott McNichols started helping his dad in 1984 by running errands for the Dung-Ho team. The elder McNichols joined Green Apple Trot in 1985, and his son, while not yet cooking, helped out.

That team - which was founded in 1982 by Mark Klunder, Uldis Sics, Lewin Wasser and Bob Hennigh - has competed every year, but 1996 since the battle began. Klunder's and Sics' sons, like the younger McNichols, also have given their time to the cause in the past.

However, this year will mark the first time in about three years any of the McNichols "boys" have competed on the Green Apple Trot team. And they are more than ready.

"Brian Scott decided this was the year to barbecue again," said his wife, Jennifer McNichols, who runs errands for the team during the competition. "They've really missed it... This is his (Brian Scott's) baby this year. He's been experimenting with Old West Spice Company spices. He's experimenting with everything he can think of."

Green Apple Trot will compete in all the categories - brisket, miscellaneous, pork, poultry, ribs and sausage - except whole animal. In all, they will cook about 40 pounds of meat.

Green Apple Trot never has won the championship. But unlike the more serious barbecuers, this is not the team members' goal.

"They don't care if they win," Jennifer McNichols said. "They are just out there to have fun."

★ ★ ★ ★ ★

After 1983, Jody Hammond's barbecue team could have changed its name to "The Flaming Goats."

"We decided to cook in the whole animal category," she said. "My husband decided to cook a goat. He and another guy built this contraption to cook in. Everything was going smoothly. When they went to check on the goat and opened the door of the cooker, flames shot into the air."

After that, the SLOB (Southern Lenexa Order of the Barbeque) team cooked a pig for the whole- animal category, and named its cooker "the cremator."

"We usually arrive in the mid-afternoon and put things on to cook Friday evening," Hammond said. Things get more serious around midnight, when teams begin cooking. Hammond said the SLOB team usually enters all the categories - brisket, miscellaneous, pork, poultry, ribs, sausage and whole animal. And, despite the goat mishap, the team tends to do well in the whole-animal category.

"There was a tiny bit of meat left after the goat flamed up for the judges to taste," she said. "Needless to say, we didn't win the whole-animal category that year."

Lenexans Ted and Donna McClure have competed in barbecue contests for 15 years throughout the Midwest and they often take home the top prize.

Yet they always have fallen short of a big goal - to win in their hometown at the Great Lenexa Barbeque Battle.

That changed in 1997.

"At last, we finally did it," said Donna McClure. "We have cooked at Lenexa for 15 years and never won the whole thing ... We've been bridesmaids several times but never the bride. We have several reserve champion awards."

The McClures' team, P.D.T. (Pretty Damn Tasty) Barbeque was crowned the grand champion last weekend. They received $1,000, a new smoker and the championship banner.

The Lenexa win was not the only first this year for the team known for "its great ribs and brisket," McClure said. P.D.T used a brand new cooker.

"It really was a good one Saturday," McClure joked.

Being mildly superstitious, however, the McClures still cooked their chicken on the same grill they've used for 15 years, and the tradition paid off.

"We got first in the chicken category," she said. "It was the first miracle of the day. Chicken is a hard category. You have to find the right table of judges who like the flavor of your chicken."

The McClures did not start out as competitors in the Lenexa Barbeque Battle. In the early years, they had less glamorous duties.

"In the beginning, the teams didn't bring their stuff (meat) to the judges," she said. "There were a few volunteers, runners, who brought food to the judges and wiped their brows (the judges') because it was so hot outside.

"We saw teams camped out under shade trees, and I said to Ted, 'Look at them. That's where we'll be next year.'"

And they have competed in Lenexa and 10 to 11 other contests every year since. Donna and Ted McClure also are original board members of the Kansas City Barbeque Society.

"We started out with a few small cookers," she said. "Then we had custom-made Oklahoma Joe's cookers, which we still have." One of their past cookers was so large it had to be pulled in a trailer.

McClure said the secret to great barbecue was good planning and consistency. P.D.T. always cooks in the four main categories - poultry, pork ribs, pork and brisket - and then enters at least one other, usually sausage.

"We don't shoot for all first or second places in all the categories," she said. "We shoot for fourths or fifths across the board, and then you're more likely to come in first overall."

The top contestants also usually are the ones who compete in at least three or four competitions each year, McClure said.

"Some teams just cook once a year in Lenexa," she said. "That's great if the judges like your stuff ... If you look at the judging score sheets, you will see the teams high on the score sheet are the ones who work the barbecue circuit."

The McClures like to hit most of the major competitions each year in Kansas, Oklahoma, Missouri, Texas and Iowa. They have won several awards over the years and competed in a few "prestigious" invitationals for larger prizes.

"Ted keeps track of the ribbons and prizes we have won," McClure said. "It's kind of like a diary (over the years)."

The popularity of the McClures' barbecue has grown over the years, especially among their friends. The couple invites them out every year on the Friday before the Lenexa competition and cooks for them.

"Once a year (Friday) we bring all our friends out to Sar-Ko-Par Trails and feed them ribs, briskets, beans and potato salad," McClure said. "We fed a ton of people this year. But Saturday we put on our judges' hats and get really serious."

Because of the high demand, the McClures now sell their barbecue for parties and events. Their menu items include baby back ribs, beef brisket, chicken and side items.

"We always are cooking slabs of ribs," she said. "There are also usually some in the freezer that can be sold and heated up."

In fact, the couple woke up early Wednesday to cook 40 slabs of ribs for the holiday weekend.

And their weekend cooking didn't stop there. They are in Osceola, Mo., this weekend seeking another championship title.

"It's a summer hobby," Donna McClure said. "Instead of going fishing or camping, we barbecue."

— Susan White

★ ★ ★ ★ ★ ★ ★ ★ ★ ★

BLUE SPRINGS BLAZE OFF
STATE CHAMPIONSHIP

The Blue Springs Blaze Off is one of scores of outstanding barbecue competitions in the Kansas City area. In 1997, former Star reporter Kim Kozlowski wrote this story that nicely captures the motives of most barbecue teams.

There's a group of guys that barbecues together in Blue Springs. But when the guys decide to put away the charcoal and smoking chips and go to a barbecue joint to eat, they all go in different directions.

Kent Edmondson goes to Arthur Bryant's Barbecue in Kansas City because he likes traditional flavor. Joe Thornburg prefers the Smokehouse in Independence because the sauce isn't too spicy. Jim Royer enjoys the Boardroom BBQ in Overland Park because he likes the sweet, molasses-style sauce. And Steve Krekeler's favorite spot is KC Masterpiece in Overland Park because he likes the restaurant's burnt ends and onion rings.

"We don't go often," Krekeler confesses, "because our attitude is, 'We can cook it better than they could.' "

Despite their different preferences, the four get together five or six times a year and smoke brisket, ribs and chicken in several local barbecue competitions. Calling themselves The Blues Brothers Bar-B-Q Team, the guys are looking forward to the American Royal Barbecue contests in October.

But for now, they're focusing on the annual Blue Springs Barbecue Blaze Off State Championship, the second-oldest barbecue contest in the Kansas City area.

Besides the meat competition, the Blaze Off features an annual salsa contest and the special Kid-Q contest. But the team's favorite part of the event is Saturday morning, when the Blue Springs High School band marches through the contest at the crack of dawn to wake up the barbecuers.

After the coals turn to ash in Blue Springs, the four will begin preparations for the American Royal competition.

Though they have earned a few awards over the years, they acknowledge they're not the most acclaimed barbecuers in Blue Springs.

"But if there was a category for having the most fun, we'd be there," Thornburg says.

At most competitions, they set up a stage, spin tunes and offer karaoke. Usually, they feature an act that they've put together, complete with air guitars.

Edmondson knows that barbecuing isn't easy. Most cooks start their fires and put meat on the grill throughout the night. As the head cook of The Blues Brothers Bar-B-Q Team, he puts their brisket on at midnight. Ribs and chicken follow a few hours later.

While he's cooking, the three others assist.

"There's a lot of prep work," Edmondson says. "You have to season the meat, wrap it. It's a team effort."

It's been an education for Royer, who learned the difference between grilling and slow barbecuing.

The Blues Brothers of barbecue (from left), Kent Edmondson, Jim Royer and Steve Krekeler.

"It's nice to know that the quality of food" is the team's focus, he says. "And it's a good Friday night party."

Krekeler likes the fact that they prepare the meat for themselves, instead of trying to impress judges.

"We cook the food the way we like it," Krekeler concludes. "Our food is good, but we don't consistently win.

If we were doing it for the money we would have quit a long time ago."

- Kim Kozlowski

★★★★★★★★★★
TAILGATING
AT ARROWHEAD

Kansas City's claim to be the Barbecue Capital of The World has been substantially validated by the tailgating tradition that precedes Chiefs games at Arrowhead stadium. The parking lot at Arrowhead fills up early on game days with fans hungry for victory and victuals.

A few dedicated devotees even show up the night before. These are the high priests of tailgating. These are the barbecue cookers. They haul their smokers in on trailers, stoke 'em up with hickory, lay in a few slabs o' ribs, a brisket or butt, or two, then sit back, sip on a toddy and let the air fill with sweet smoke, like incense at high Mass.

When you read these three tailgating tales from *The Star* you'll be reminded that the word "fan" comes from the word "fanatic."

WE CAME HERE TO PARTAKE

In space N-43, the group in black and gold was eyeing the red and gold paint-splattered van over in N-45.

"We may have to go over there and do something about that," Brian McCloy told his buddies, his eyes narrowing to slits.

McCloy pointed to a dummy dressed in Pittsburgh Steelers colors, hanging from a pole above the van. Half a dozen arrows pierced the dummy's chest, and a Chiefs flag loomed above.

Then, laughing, the Pittsburgh man said: "Oh, well. This is all just part of the atmosphere.

"And we came here to partake of it."

So did nearly 80,000 other dedicated and radical fans, who braved the blustery, drizzly elements and began setting up camp when the gates opened at 4 p.m.

Many hours before a 17-7 Chiefs loss quieted the crowd, it was time for "Monday Night Football" at Arrowhead Stadium, and the fan feeding frenzy that precedes such occasions.

"Tonight, we're feasting on pork," said Rick Salinas of Olathe, the driver of the van with the dummy on top.

When told that some Steelers fans were offended at his work of art, Salinas pounded his chest. "Bring 'em on!" he boasted.

"Are we crazy?" he then asked, to no one in particular. "Most definitely. But Monday night football is a big deal. The whole country's going to be watching. And people are riled up and ready to go!"

So ready, in fact, that there was already a long line at the portable toilets just 15 minutes after the gates opened.

Closer to the stadium, a group of fans feasted on shrimp and dip and sipped on muas.

That's right. Muas. Pronounced *moo-ahs*.

"This is our special drink we created that is named for (former Chiefs nose tackle) Dan Saleaumua," explained Judi Walker of Lawrence, who was tailgating with friends and relatives from Salina, Kan., and Olathe. "This is a tradition. We drink these before every game for good luck."

The drink, she and her colleagues said, is made of tropical schnapps and orange juice.

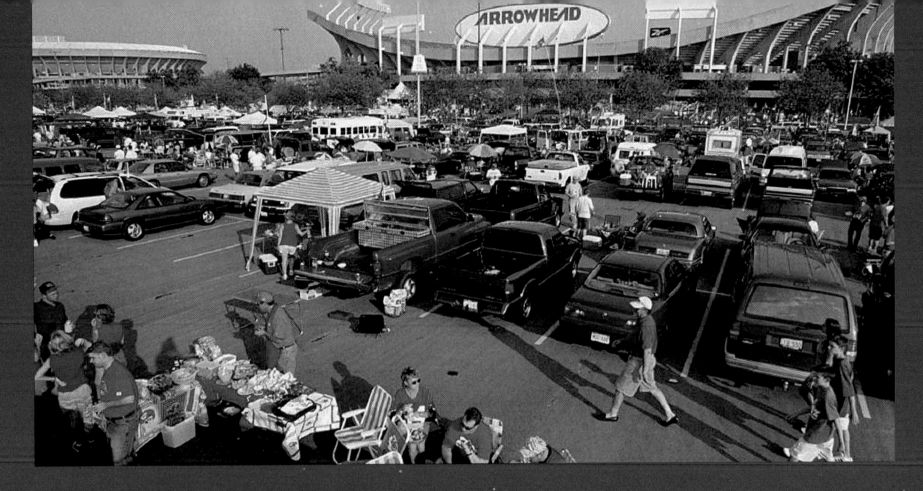

Some fans found other ways of warming themselves, by snuggling in sleeping bags or hovering around barbecue smokers. Other not-so-adventuresome ones sat in their vehicles until time to head to the stadium.

As usual, the parking lot took on a carnivallike atmosphere as music blared, fans roamed in bizarre get-ups and the aroma of every kind of barbecued meat imaginable filled the nostrils and lingered on hair and clothing.

Two hours before kickoff, a plane flew overhead with a banner that said: "Julie will you marry me? Love Danny!"

As game time approached, Rusty Anderson and his brother-in-law Gene Myracle, both of Leavenworth, headed toward the stadium, drawing stares with every step.

The two had shaved the sides of their heads, then painted the stubble on top bright green with white stripes through it.

"That represents the green turf, and the white is the yard lines," Anderson said.

They had painted the rest of their faces to look like football helmets.

"This is airbrushed on," Anderson said. "We're hoping it will wash off."

Why did they do it? "We want to get on national television," he said.

Nearby, in Lot D-16, a four-piece band had attracted an audience as it played everything from rock to country to - yes, even the Macarena.

A few parking stalls down, four Jackson County sheriff's deputies enjoyed the music as they filled their plates with a wide assortment of delectables before heading to work inside the stadium.

"We started out with a bowl of chicken noodle soup, then a bowl of chili," said Deputy J.R. Leaming. "Then we went over to Lot E and had pizza and shrimp cocktail, met (former Steeler) Lynn Swann, got his autograph, then came over here. Now we're having shrimp, crab legs and linguine with clam sauce."

Been crashing a few tailgates, have you, deputies?

"Oh, no," Leaming politely replied. "We call this community policing."

— Judy Thomas
October 1996

SACRIFICIAL FOODS

Joyce Huston and her friend Dixie Givan arrived early at Arrowhead Stadium for the Chiefs' last exhibition game against the Buffalo Bills. After all, the two women and their husbands, Winton Huston and Ken Givan, had a lot of work to do in the three hours before kickoff.

There was the 10-foot square tent, Huston's Huddle, to erect and decorate with a color-coordinated decor that would make plenty of interior decorators jealous. There was the red table and chairs to set up, the red tablecloth to lay out, the red plates and red glasses and Chiefs silverware to set out from the makeshift toolbox painted with arrowheads.

Then there was the Chiefs helmet grill to fire up, using a Chiefs oven mitt to remove the hot cover, of course. Meanwhile, there were Chiefs umbrellas, Chiefs shakers, a Chiefs decanter and the Chiefs helmet nut dish to haul out of the Chiefs minivan and display.

It wouldn't be a Chiefs game without a tailgate party. Or 10,000.

"It's more important than the game," tailgater John McMaster of Lenexa said.

"If you don't do it, you're not a Chiefs fan," B.J. Miller of Roeland Park added.

The enthusiasm of the Kansas City fans for their Chiefs, and for their tailgating, has been well documented. They've been featured in *Sports Illustrated* magazine and in football highlight videotapes by the NFL. So well-known have they become that as many as eight NFL teams, including expansion clubs and Jacksonville, have sent crews of team officials to observe the Chiefs' pregame operations for tips and ideas.

Fox TV announcer John Madden, an expert on food as well as football, ranks the Kansas City tailgaters among the best in the country.

"There's something about Kansas City," Madden said during his visit for the home opener against the New York Giants. "It's very bright and festive. It kind of smells like tailgating. If you were to pick an All-Tailgate Team, Kansas City would be one of 'em, along with Green Bay and Chicago. The big thing is, they have enough space and the right type of people and the right type of food."

From burgers and beer to prime rib and champagne, there's a little something for everyone before the game.

"It's part of a large play book of operations to make the game-day experience more than a game," said Tim Connolly, the former Chiefs executive vice president and chief operating officer who is given credit for turning the Chiefs games into mini-festivals. "Tailgating has taken on a life of its own. It's almost a competitive event in itself. This is what Kansas City is known for."

Indeed, Chiefs officials estimate that as many as 2,000 fans come just to tailgate. Many of these tailgaters don't even have tickets to the game.

Jamie Cameron is one of those people. She and 10 or 12 friends load the food and drinks into the car, along with a television and portable generator.

"We couldn't get tickets," she explained. "So we just decided to do this. It's fun. We go the whole nine yards."

So do other fans who do have tickets.

Bob Davila Jr. of Lee's Summit and his family the distinction of being among the first fans to tailgate at the Chiefs games. Bob (Nick) Davila Sr. has had season tickets since 1964, and the Davila family has been tailgating in parking lot G since 1975 or 1976.

"People stared at us like we were freaks at first," Bob Davila Jr. said, laughing. "We'd bring a lot of homemade Hispanic American food, and people wanted to know if we'd sell stuff."

Ted DeWolf and friends had another idea people wanted to share. They brought their own 7-foot-high plywood porta-john to the game.

Larry and Kay Wichmann of St. Joseph insist that anyone attending the games and/or tailgates with them wear red.

"We've dug into our closets for Chiefs sweat shirts if they aren't wearing red," Larry Wichmann said. "We demand that they do that."

Tim Johnson of Brookside doesn't always get to the game, but he, too, has a game-day ritual.

"I start at 5:30 or 6 a.m. with four or five cups of strong coffee," Johnson said. "Then I go outside and fly my Chiefs flag. I'm sort of a Chiefs fanatic. It's all a big release for me, kind of a spiritual thing. Sometimes I get so excited I feel like throwing up. Sometimes I do.

"For every game, I make sacrificial foods. Like opening day this year, I made a smoked turkey. A turkey is kind of a dumb Seahawk, right? Last year we had Cajun food when they opened against New Orleans.

"I'm very superstitious. If I have to work and I can't go to the game, they usually lose."

What Jimmy Manuel of Kansas City, Kan., enjoys is the bond that forms among tailgaters.

"You don't have to worry about racial things," he said. "It's all about the Chiefs. There's no color barrier at a tailgate. It is one big happy family."

Even the players have been known to take part in their own versions of tailgate parties after the games while waiting for traffic to clear.

"Everybody is hungry and thirsty, so we get together to do our own thing," linebacker Tracy Simien said. "Everybody else is having a good time. Why shouldn't we?"

—Mary Schmitt
November 1995

AS IF DRAWN BY SMOKE

Smoke pours through the towering lights of Arrowhead, making the stadium look from afar like a huge kettle of boiling soup.

It's 6 p.m. Monday, two hours before the kickoff of the Raiders game. Chiefs fans have come home to dinner.

Thousands of tailgaters gather around barbecue smokers and grills in the parking lot and the grassy hills, turning the home of the Chiefs into a city of backyards.

But the boundaries are vague, as if drawn by smoke.

Tailgaters drift from one parking space to another, sharing sauce and spirit. The air is thick with aroma. Here there are no strangers. Wear red and they'll feed you barbecue like you're family.

If you don't eat it, they'll think you're a Raiders fan.

"But we would feed you anyway," Dave Gallagher said.

He and a crew of 25 or so work buddies and family were enjoying a feast of bratwurst, baked beans, potato salad and pumpkin pie.

"Shoot, look at this," he said, pointing to his 11-year-old son, Eric, who was wearing a Raiders shirt.

"I cover him up with a Chiefs blanket every night, but he won't come around," Gallagher said.

Most tailgaters are old hands. Ask them how long they've been doing the pre-game barbecues and they look to the sky, trying to remember the season they started.

Some can't. Others can tell you the game and the score.

They say that tailgate parties are their way of being part of the game.

"The game is in there," lawyer Irv Ness said, pointing to the stadium. "But it's out here, too. It's all part of coming to a Chiefs game."

His group numbered about 30. Other tailgate parties are smaller. For some it's a table for two. Maybe a couple of porterhouse steaks and a bottle of red wine.

And what to cook?

Well, the old-timers tell you that the art of tailgating cannot be rushed.

"You start with hot dogs and hamburgers," Judy O'Connor said. "Simple things. Then you work yourself up to fancier dishes."

She's learned the art. Monday, it was lemon marinated chicken breasts for her bunch.

"We've graduated," her husband, Phil Gellott, said smiling.

Game day starts early for tailgaters, especially for Monday night games.

First object of the day is to figure out how to leave work early. They like to be at the stadium at least by 5 p.m.

For some, it's a simple task: They lie to their boss.

Those people asked that their names not be used for this story.

Others, such as Gary Lowe, could be honest.

"I'm a judge," Lowe said.

Lowe, an administrative Social Security judge, and a group of about 30 friends are regular tailgaters and season-ticket holders.

"The only way we wouldn't do this is if we couldn't get a fire going," Lowe said. "We're hooked. It's almost like a religion."

—Donald Bradley
October 1991

Below: James Thomas (left) enjoys barbecue with his buddies at a Chiefs home game.

CHAPTER FOUR

BARBECUE FOR
BACKYARD BEGINNERS

It's about time we actually *define* barbecue. What barbecue *is* is the indirect cooking of meat with hardwood coals at (relatively) low heat for a long time. The mantra of barbecue cookers is "low and slow."

What barbecue is *not* is grilling. Grilling is direct cooking over wood or coals. Grilling is fast and fiery.

When people cook burgers or steak in the backyard they sometimes say they are "barbecuing." They are not. They are grilling. Grilling and barbecuing have as much in common as boiling and baking. They are both cooking methods. But that's as far as it goes. They're not the same thing.

Barbecue infuses meat with a rich and complex smoky flavor. The meat is thoroughly tenderized by the low and slow cooking process while retaining its natural moisture.

Grilling cooks meat directly over flames or intense heat from burning wood or charcoal. This sears the meat, sealing in the meat's flavor and moisture.

Both are good. But they're not the same.

In *The Great American Barbeque Instruction Book*, barbecue is defined as, "Meat cooked in the dry heat of wood coals at temperatures about the boiling point of water." Other techniques, such as roasting (cooking in an oven at 250-400 degrees), or broiling (cooking under a heat element at 500-700 degrees) can produce wonderful results. And meat cooked by any of these methods my be flavored by marinades, rubs, bastes and finishing sauces. However - and this is critical - the addition of barbecue sauce to a piece of meat does *not* transform that meat into barbecue.

You'll find so-called recipes for "barbecue" in lots of cookbooks that call for roasting, or in some cases *boiling* (!), ribs and coating them in sauce.

Folks, this ain't barbecue.

Barbecue does not in fact require sauce at all. Just as you can have cake without icing, it is perfectly acceptable to have barbecue without sauce.

Furthermore, there are no "recipes" for barbecue. There is one technique for making barbecue, but this is not a recipe. There are very few variations on this one fundamental technique.

In this section we will provide you with basic information you may use in making barbecue at home. The emphasis is on the word *basic*. There's nothing fancy here. Fancy is not what barbecue is about.

Q

NO MATTER HOW YOU SPELL IT

You know about Kansas City barbecue, and Texas barbecue and Carolina barbecue and all the rest, but can you *spell* barbecue?

Sure you can, because in the spelling, at least, anything goes.

Local barbecue aficionado Ardie Davis says he figures there are at least 25 ways to spell it. When he's in other cities he checks out the barbecue - and the spellings. Some years ago he founded the Diddy-Wa-Diddy National Barbecue Sauce Contest (that first year it was held on his back patio), which since has become part of the American Royal barbecue contest.

Here's a list (incomplete, we're sure) of the variations on that word that starts with a "b" and ends with a "q" sound and is so big around these parts. The commentary is ours.

Barbecue. The version dictionaries prefer, which is an excellent reason to go with something else. Dictionaries, being precise and unwavering, couldn't possibly understand something that drips and requires a towelette.

Barbeque. It looks right, but it sneaks a "q" in there. This is the spelling favored by the Kansas City Barbeque Society. Why? "It's a why-be-normal thing," says Carolyn Wells, the group's executive director. "We like to be a little off-center so we use the less traditional spelling."

Bar-B-Q. Gates, Snead's, Zarda and most KC joints, in fact, like this spelling best. It's short and sweet but still phonetically correct: Bar-B-Q equals barbecue. Another variation? Break out the lower case letters: Bar-b-q.

Bar-B-Que. This would be a good name for a ranch, don'tcha think?

BBQ or bbq. Heard those radio spots for KCP&L ("How Kansas City Are You?") in which a champion speller has a go at some Cowtown words? This is how he spells it. B-B-Q. Soon to be an ABC sitcom: "Two B's, a Q and a Hyphen."

(Well, OK, there are two hyphens, but who's counting?)

Barbee-Que. Davis has run across this one. You probably could spell it Barbie-Que, but we doubt barbecue has ever passed Barbie's lips. Then again, maybe wolfing barbecue is what's given her a fuller figure.

Bar-b-cue. Need a cue to chow down? And ... action!

Bar-Be-Cue. Pretty bar-be-cute.

Barbq. Wethinks it needs a hyphen somewhere.

Bar-BQ. Saucy!

Davis prefers the standard spelling: barbecue. There's one good practical reason for producers of sauce, rubs and the like to play it straight, he says: A too-cutesy spelling may end up being missed in food brokers' databases - which could mean your product doesn't make it onto as many grocery shelves as it might otherwise.

Wells and Davis agree that rib joints may sometimes go with shorter spellings to save money (fewer letters on a sign, fewer bucks).

Then again, maybe none of this really matters. Show-Me-ites and others will probably argue till the end of time about how the state's name is pronounced (Missou-REE? Missou-RUH?); Kansas Citians will forever disagree about whether the Seville-styled shopping district is the PlAAA-za or the PIAH-za.

As for barbecue...

"It doesn't matter how you spell it," Wells says. "It's still the hottest thing going."

- Tim Engle

BBQ ON THE WWW

There are more on-line resources for barbecuers than there are empty beer cans in the parking lot at Arrowhead after a tailgate party. Here are some of the best:

First, try **www.smokering.net.** This is the home page for The Smoke Ring, a "BBQ Neighborhood Website" with over 465 participating member sites. On the list are restaurants, vendors, entrepreneurs, state and local barbecue associations, and personal home pages of barbecue enthusiasts and teams. This site is good for repeat visits.

A useful all-purpose barbecue site is **www.barbecuen.com**. My favorite feature of this site is the column by "Smoky" Hale, an extraordinarily knowledgeable and gifted writer.

The Kansas City Bar-B-Q Connection is located at **www.rbjb.com/rbjb/bbq.htm**. This is a straightforward and practical site and a good way to access other local barbecue online resources.

If you're serious about your barbecue cooking, some indispensable information may be found at **www.velvitoil.com/Survive.** This site is home to the BBQ FAQs, which have been accumulating for years and offer responses to both simple and complex cooking questions. Many of the answers are provided by some of the most trusted personalities in barbecue. This site is not pretty, but it's pretty helpful.

My favorite all-round barbecue Website is The Lexington Collection, located at **www.ibiblio.org/lineback/lex.htm**. This site features fine writing, well-researched history, nicely-organized links, and useful tips for amateur cooks. It might be the perfect barbecue Website if it weren't dedicated specifically to *North Carolina* barbecue.

- D.W.

- NOTE -

Internet sites, like the value of Internet stocks, come and go. All of these sites were operational at the time this book was published, and we expect they will remain so. However, occasionally web sites are shut down or web addresses are changed.

★ ★ ★ ★ ★

EQUIPMENT

There are three basic cookers that may be used in making barbecue: good old Weber-type kettle grills, water smokers and wood smokers.

I used a Weber for years and over time learned to make wonderful barbecue with it. I've never used a water smoker, but some of my best friends use 'em and they swear by 'em. These days I'm using a big beastly Bandera unit from New Braunfels that my wife bought me. It's awesome.

WATER SMOKERS

Water smokers allow the barbecue cook to put meat in the smoker and more or less leave it alone, checking on it only every hour or so. Most are less expensive than wood smokers and require less time maintaining the cooking temperatures.

Water smokers are either electric or charcoal 'fired.' The heat source is located below the meat. To obtain smoke, water-soaked wood chunks are placed on or near the heat sources, which causes the wood to smolder and circulate within the cooking chamber.

Water smokers also use water (thus the name) which is placed either directly above or adjacent to the heat source and creates steam, which combines with the smoke to keep the meat moist while cooking.

Top: The classic Weber grill.
Middle: A water smoker
Bottom: A wood smoker with offset firebox.
Thanks to Strasser Hardware.

WOOD SMOKERS

A wood smoker uses wood, charcoal or a combination of the two as its cooking fuel.

The basic components of a wood smoker are the firebox, the cooking chamber and the chimney. The main work of the cook (and it *is* a lot of work) is to maintain temperature (fire), and to maintain a consistent flow of heat and smoke through the cooking chamber and adequate exhaust through the chimney.

Smokers are heavy, sometimes weighing 200 pounds or more, and unless they are mounted on a trailer, are not very portable.

The firebox is usually located to one side of the smoker. This is because wood smokers are primarily for cooking *indirectly*. This method prevents the meat from being seared by direct heat. Indirect cooking requires less frequent turning and more cooking time because the meat is being barbecued at roughly 225 degrees.

Wood, or wood coals or charcoal are burned in the firebox, which has an adjustable air intake found in its door. There is also a grate in the firebox that allows air to flow under the wood/charcoal to fuel the fire. Heat and smoke flow from the firebox into the cooking chamber and then around and over the meat and out the chimney.

GEORGE GURLEY

FIDDLING WITH MY DAMPERS

I f you can get past former *Star* book critic George Gurley's outrageous first sentence, I think you'll enjoy his ode to a smoker, which appeared in *The Star* in August of 1993.

I was never that crazy about barbecue. The Calvin Trillin School of Barbecue Mysticism bored me. The Midwestern equation of barbecue and virtue annoyed me. Above all, compared to real cuisine, barbecue seemed crude.

Nevertheless, from the moment I laid eyes on Oklahoma Joe's Bar-B-Q Smoker, I had to have one.

It was an arresting object, utterly self-contained, complete. It's lines suggested a steam locomotive, with associations of romance and workhorse power.

It proclaimed the confidence of "The Little Engine that Could." ("I think I can, I know I can.") I found myself thinking, "If I had a smoker like that, I too could climb mountains. I would be a professional. People would look up to me, I would win respect."

I knew that nursing a desire rather than acting on it could be disastrous for mental health, so I ran out and got myself one of Joe's Oklahoma Traditions smokers without thinking about my high cholesterol or my indifference to barbecue.

It was everything I'd hoped for. Made of quarter-inch steel, it looked indestructible, bullet-proof. It took two men and three boys to lift it off the truck.

It actually had its own serial number on a small brass plate. The fluid, immaculate welding seams spoke of craftsmanship and ought to have been signed by the artist.

My model consisted of a cylindrical smoke box joined to a larger smoking chamber from which a jaunty smokestack protruded like a flexed arm. The overall effect was: "heavy-duty," "manly," "no nonsense."

At once I began smoking meats far in excess of my family's needs and with disappointing results. Chicken came out oversmoked and undercooked. My first brisket could have served as Joe Montana's shoulder pad.

Apparently there was an art to smoking meat. Instead of being transformed into a confident, can-do guy, I plunged to new lows of self-doubt and began to think about seeking professional help.

Running into Lindsay Shannon on a stairway, I flung myself on him like the Ancient Mariner.

"Why can't I keep my fire going?" I cried. "Why does my brisket come out so tough?" Shannon - proprietor of B-B's Lawnside Bar-B-Que and host of a blues show on the radio - regarded me with a mixture of sympathy and wariness. Did he think I was trying to muscle in on his turf, steal his secrets?

He told me how he'd started off with a homemade smoker on a grocery cart, how even the pros who compete in the American Royal Barbecue Contest sometimes burn their meat and he generously whispered the key to cooking brisket.

"It takes time," he said.

These days I can often be found beside my smoker, fiddling with my dampers, cleaning out my grease trap, laying a fresh stick of apple wood on the coals. My own flesh is beginning to smell smoke-cured.

I'm happy to report that I'm getting better. I'm even beginning to develop a taste for barbecue. I consult a barbecue bible that celebrates the joys of pigging out on lard-laced meat and implies that to kill a vegetarian is justifiable homicide. I've tapped into a barbecue support group.

Modern man has been rendered superfluous by machines. He has abdicated his role in the family. He no longer returns with dead animals from the hunt. What does he have left besides the smoker?

When I stand by my Oklahoma Traditions smoker like Vulcan at his forge, I feel there's still a justification for my existence - keeper of the sacred coals, provider of the ribs, spreader of the sauce.

—George Gurley

GUIDE TO
SMOKING WOODS

★ ★ ★ ★ ★ ★ ★ ★ ★ ★

ALDER

Slightly sweet

Best for fish

ALMOND

Sweet and nutty. Good all-around wood, but hard to find.

Works well with most meats

APPLE

Sweet, rich, fruity smoke. Preferred by many of the champions at the American Royal Barbecue.

Superb for pork, ribs and whole hogs

APRICOT

Mild and sweet. May be used in with stronger woods for balance.

Great for poultry and fish.

ASH

Light, but pleasant-tasting smoke.

Better for fish and red meat than for poultry.

BIRCH

Much like maple, but milder.

Works well with pork and poultry.

CHERRY

Fruity, sweet, milder than apple.

A favorite with a few loyalists, cherry works well with beef. It will tend to darken the meat more than other woods will.

GRAPE VINES

Similar to other fruit woods. More popular in California.

Use with chicken or game birds

HICKORY

The "king" of smoking woods. Preferred by most barbecue restaurants. Produces a strong, smoky bacon/hamlike flavor. Some cookers feel that hickory can be overpowering and therefore prefer to mix other kinds of wood in with their fire.

Great with all meats.

MAPLE

Mildly sweet and smoky. Imparts a baconlike flavor.

Best with pork.

MULBERRY

Sweet and mild.

Good for game birds, poultry and pork.

OAK

The "queen" of smoking woods. Straightforward, bold and slightly sweet flavor. Used in lots of barbecue joints.

Perfect for all meats.

PEACH

Slightly sweet and earthy.

Good for most meat, and mixes well with harsher woods.

PEAR

Like a milder apple smoke.

Works nicely on game birds, poultry, and pork.

PECAN

The "pope" of smoking woods. Considered by many barbecue cooks to be the best. Produces a rich, hickorylike flavor, yet is not as harsh as hickory. Pecan burns cool, so is ideal for the "low and slow" technique.

Ideal for all meats.

PLUM

Mild and sweeter.

Good for fish and chicken.

WALNUT

Strong smoky flavor. Usually used with milder, sweeter woods such as apple, cherry, or pecan.

Best for beef and stronger tasting game meats.

Note: Mesquite has become a popular cooking wood in restaurants and backyards. Do not use it to barbecue. It burns hot, making temperature control difficult. Mesquite also can produce a bitter taste when used in smoking. It is much better suited for use in grilling.

Fairlane BBQ Wood is one of the Kansas City area's premier suppliers of hardwood chunks for barbecue. Fairlane's wood is conveniently packaged in large, rugged plastic bags and is readily available at area hardware stores and even at some butcher shops and supermarkets. Oak, hickory, apple, cherry and pecan are the most popular varieties Fairlane sells.

★ ★ ★ ★ ★ ★ ★ ★ ★

FRANKLY SPEAKING

There are only two things you really need for barbecue: a hunk of tough meat and a fire of hardwood. Anything else you might add is, well, just something else you might add. And whatever it is it's unnecessary. That includes rubs, sauces and anything and everything in between. Your meat you get from your butcher. (You do *know* your butcher, don't you?) And your wood you get from Frank Schloegel III.

Frank owns Southside Patio and Wood Co. in Kansas City, Kansas. There are other places to get wood, of course. But they don't have Frank, a fast-talking, cigar-chomping, BS-detecting, 59-year-old redheaded raconteur with a gleam in his eye, who, on the off chance he'll actually be there, is reason enough to stop in for a load of hickory.

Frank Schloegel Sr. — that'd be Frank III's grandfather — started the business back in 1912. He was an entrepreneurial German immigrant looking for a way to make a living in America, so he leased a vacant lot just south of Kelly's bar in Westport and had a load of coal dumped on it and started selling the coal retail. Southside Coal Co. is what he called it.

"He ran the business out of his pocket," Frank III says. "He was always on the move, always making deals."

Apparently it worked. Well enough, at least, that when it was time, there was enough of a business there that it could be passed along to Frank Jr., Frank III's father.

But by then things had changed.

"My dad used to tell us how, in like one month's time, he went from selling so many hundreds of carloads of coal to like *20*," Frank recalls. "Everybody started heating with gas, and that was the end of the coal business."

Frank Jr. must have seen the end coming, however, because by the time the coal biz had burned out, Southside was, among other things, already selling firewood. Quite a bit of it, in fact, to the barbecue joints in town, who were pretty iffy customers. There were lots of them and they bought lots of wood, but they didn't always pay on time. Sometimes they didn't pay at all.

But after all those deliveries and all those sales calls to all those rib joints, Frank Jr. must have picked up a few pointers, because after a while he was turning out some pretty tasty barbecue himself.

"I remember my dad would smoke batches of ribs and take 'em up the hill to Kelly's and they would buy 'em from him," Frank III says. "That went on for quite a while. Then one day, the health department came by and told my dad,

★ ★ ★ ★ ★ ★ ★ ★ ★

'We've had our eye on you and we know there's no way you're eating all those ribs you're cooking. And we know where they're goin'.' They told him to quit it. So that was the end of that. I'll never forget that day. It was a Friday."

Frank Jr.'s mastery of barbecued ribs was apparently known to more than just the health department, however. Soon the folks from Hasty Bake ovens approached him with an offer to travel around the country with their salesmen showing restaurants how to make barbecue with the company's ovens.

"My dad was pretty much a family man, though," Frank III says. "He didn't want to be gone that much, so he turned 'em down."

But that wasn't the end of the Schloegel family involvement in barbecue.

Eventually the lease on the Westport lot ran out and the Schloegels moved the business a couple of times, eventually landing on a two-acre parcel on Merriam Lane. They continued to supply joints in town with hickory and oak while dabbling in other lines of business, such as topsoil and bricks.

The evidence of these other ventures is scattered around Southside's scrubby tract. Between huge piles of oak and hickory are small heaps of building and landscape materials, tiles, blocks and bricks.

"You wouldn't necessarily know it to look at it," concedes Frank III, "But we've actually cleaned the place up quite a bit. And eventually all the bricks and other stuff will be gone. We can't compete in those businesses any more."

These days Southside sells mostly to Gates, Hayward's and B.B.'s Lawnside. They move about 100 cords of wood per month. Gates alone buys at least three cords per week for each of its locations.

Most of the wood comes from small-time farmers in the Ozarks. Schloegel says that he has 10 to 15 suppliers, but only four or five he can count on.

"There's quite a bit of turn-over," he says. "Lots of these guys are crooked. They'll try to cheat you anyway they can. Most of 'em think it's going to be easy money. But the truth is that there's hardly any money in it at all. It's lots of work. Lot's of loading and unloading. It takes its toll on your equipment and on your body. It's heavy and you can get cut. These farmers figure that it's good extra income because they've got wood on their property and they've got the trucks. But a load of wood probably weighs 5,000 pounds and they're haulin' it way up here. It'll wear your truck out fast. And when they figure out that they're gonna need that truck to haul their grain to market, they usually come to the conclusion that they don't want to be in the wood business anymore."

Schloegel explains that frequently he'll cut a deal with some outfit to supply him with so many cords of wood for so many months, but then after a couple of weeks they simply don't show up anymore.

"Lots of these big, strong, young guys will get all excited about cuttin' and sellin' wood when it's winter," he says. "Then in the summer they lose their enthusiasm when they have to deal with the snakes and the heat."

Southside sells only hardwood. Mostly hickory, but some oak and occasionally other woods, such as pecan, cherry and maple.

"We used to sell lots of firewood to residential customers," Schloegel says. "But most of the new houses only have gas fireplaces. Funny thing is, when gas prices started going up so high, lots of these homeowners started wishing they had a regular ol' wood fireplace again."

Though he sells his wood mostly to commercial barbecue establishments, he also sells wood bagged up in smaller quantities to amateur barbecue cookers.

"On the weekends when they hold those barbecue contests like the Royal or the one in Lenexa, we sell out," he says. "They all come in here asking for their favorite woods and each one of 'em has their own little story to tell about the contest. They all have their special rubs. Then maybe this guy uses cherry wood exclusively and he's convinced it's going to make a difference. And then this other guy, well, he's so sure this is gonna be his year he can just feel it."

On Saturdays the folks at Southside fire up their own smokers — two beautiful brick monsters that squat on their main building's front patio — and barbecue briskets, butts and hams.

"We're gettin' ready to expand that part of the business," Frank explains. "We're gonna clean the place up a little and sell barbecue as take out only and for catering and gift baskets. We've already got our own sauce."

He pulls a bottle of Woodyard Bar-B-Que sauce from a carton.

"There's not much money to be made in the barbecue business," concludes Frank Schloegel III. "But you don't do it for the money. You do it because your father did it before you. You do it for love."

BEEF CUTS FOR BARBECUE

★ ★ ★ ★ ★ ★ ★ ★ ★ ★

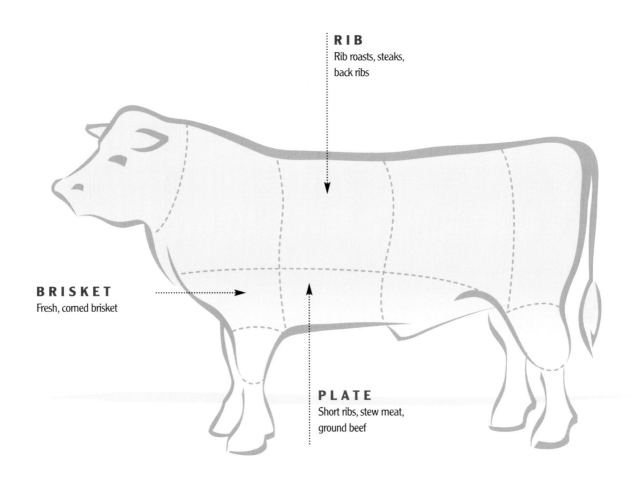

RIB
Rib roasts, steaks,
back ribs

BRISKET
Fresh, corned brisket

PLATE
Short ribs, stew meat,
ground beef

★ ★ ★ ★ ★ ★ ★ ★ ★ ★

BARBECUE
PORK & POULTRY

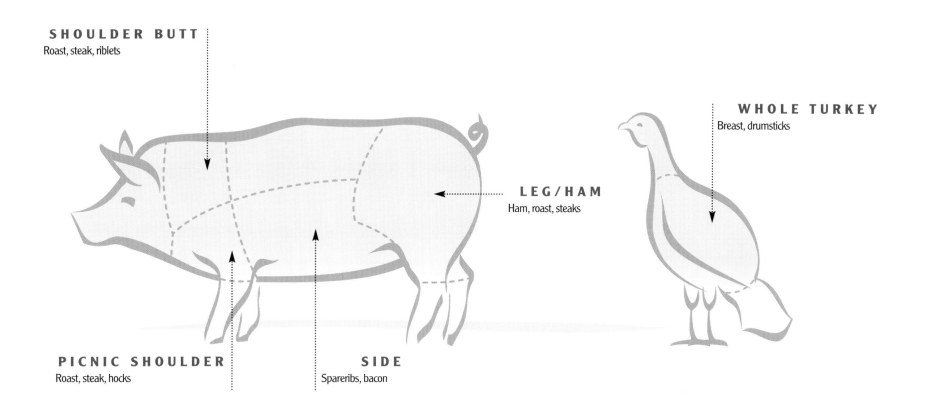

SHOULDER BUTT
Roast, steak, riblets

WHOLE TURKEY
Breast, drumsticks

LEG/HAM
Ham, roast, steaks

PICNIC SHOULDER
Roast, steak, hocks

SIDE
Spareribs, bacon

OTHER GREAT SOURCES FOR MEAT IN KANSAS CITY

Mr. Prime Beef	Bichelmeyer's	Snow Meat Market	Rancher's Gourmet Meats
1499 SW Market	704 Cheyenne	515 N. 6th	12060 Blue Valley Parkway
Lee's Summit, Missouri	Kansas City, Kansas	Kansas City, Kansas	Overland Park, Kansas

TO MARKET, TO MARKET

MCGONIGLE'S FOOD STORE

Kansas City may not be a cowtown, but it was. Meat made this place. Kansas City is even the namesake of prime cuts of meat, in spite of anything New York may have to say on the subject. Kansas Citians know from meat.

As we've already established, the only two things you need for barbecue are wood and meat. Even so, fancy frou frou meat boutiques are not where you go for your briskets and your butts. Fancy is not what barbecue is all about. When Arthur Bryant used the word "fancy" he looked as if he'd just bit into an apple and found half a worm. He understood that barbecue is about making do with what you've got.

The best place to go for meat for your barbecue is your local grocery store. And if your local grocery store happens to be McGonigle's, well, then you're one of the lucky ones.

McGonigle's Food Store, at 79th Street and Ward Parkway, has been in business for fifty years. During that time grocery giants such as A&P, Kroger and Safeway have tried to crush this little market.

"But they're all gone, and we're still here," said Mike McGonigle. "We must be doing something right."

The McGonigle family got into the grocery business in 1951 when Mike's father, William E.

McGonigle, purchased an existing store on the site. In those days there was a neighborhood grocery every five blocks, Mike McGonigle says.

"That was the way people shopped then. You walked to your local market for the things you needed that day. When the superstores moved to town, it was real tough for neighborhood stores."

McGonigle's has been blessed with a good location. But when the city rerouted Ward Parkway in the 1970s, the construction mess and detours "nearly shut us down," McGonigle recalls.

But the little store survived. Today it specializes in the very things the big supermarkets find it hard to deliver: service and personal relationships with customers.

That's what keeps Meg Duggan coming back. "They have nice clean aisles and fresh meat," Duggan says. "They're friendly here and they know me."

Responding to customer needs, the store has expanded over the years to include a full line of meats, fresh seafood and a deli department.

When his father retired in 1986, McGonigle bought the store. He takes pride in the fact that his customers come not just from the surrounding neighborhood, but from throughout the metro area.

"Trust and loyalty," McGonigle says. "That's

what people respond to."

That, and good meat.

Meat has become a specialty for McGonigle's and they've earned a reputation for being the best retail butchers in town.

"I had a guy walk in the store once who wanted a slab of St. Louis-style beef baby back spareribs," McGonigle says. "I just laughed. What else can you do? He had four or five different ribs mixed into one sentence. And he wanted one slab of them. I said, 'I can give you a slab of each, but I don't think I can cross-breed the cows and pigs that way!' "

You get the feeling, though, that if he could, he would.

"We listen to what our customers want and we try to give it to them," he says. "That's what we do best."

★ ★ ★ ★ ★ ★ ★ ★ ★ ★

BARBECUE TECHNIQUE

STEP-BY-STEP

Barbecue requires a certain attention to detail and a significant investment of time, but it doesn't require a big beast of a smoker. Your humble kettle grill will do just fine, and on page 103 we'll show you how to use it to produce great results. If, however, you are lucky enough to have a wife as wonderful as mine, she'll buy you a big beast of a smoker to congratulate you for getting your boss to agree to let you write a book about barbecue.

Rub or marinade, wrap tightly and refrigerate

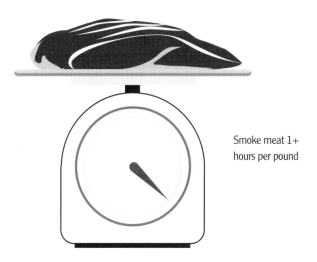

Smoke meat 1+ hours per pound

1. Season the meat with a rub or a marinade the day before. I say the day before, as opposed to the night before, because you might actually have to start cooking in the middle of the night, and if you only started the seasoning process a few hours before, that won't be enough time. If you plan to eat at 5:00 p.m. on a Sunday, get your seasoning started sometime Saturday morning.

If you use a rub, first rinse the meat then pat it dry with paper towels. Liberally apply the rub by sprinkling it all over the meat on both sides. Then wrap it tightly in a few layers of plastic wrap and stick it in the fridge.

If you use a marinade, put the meat in a watertight plastic container large enough to hold both the meat and plenty of marinade. Cover the meat entirely with marinade, and then some. Stick it in the fridge.

2. The weight of the meat will determine when you should start cooking. Allow for an hour, or more, of cooking time for every pound of meat. So, if you have an 8-pound brisket, plan on 8-12 hours in the smoker. Remember, "low and slow" is the key. You'll be cooking at a relatively low temperature — about 225 degrees — but you'll be cooking for a long time.

So, assuming an 8-pound brisket, if you plan to serve dinner at 5 on Sunday afternoon, you should get your meat in the smoker no later than 5 a.m. Sunday morning. This allows plenty of cooking time, plus some time get the meat off the grill and let it sit for a while before you carve it up nice and pretty.

If the meat gets done before you're ready to serve, wrap it up tight in foil and put it in the oven on the "warm" setting. It won't lose any flavor. Chef Paul Kirk says it's a good idea to lay some apple slices on top of the meat when you do this. It'll help keep it moist.

Graphics by: Gentry Mullen

Remove meat from refrigerator
1 hour before smoking

4. Fill the drip pan in the smoker with apple juice, or beer, or water with herbs and spices of your choice, or with just plain water. This will help keep the cooking process moist and cool. You'll probably have to add more liquid to the pan during cooking so keep some handy.

Fill drip pan with liquid and place under grate in smoker

3. Take the meat out of the refrigerator about an hour before you put it in the smoker. There's a complicated scientific explanation having to do with condensation for why this is important, but letting the meat warm up a bit (to room temperature) before you start cooking it will help prevent the build-up of creosote on the inside walls of your smoker. Creosote is nasty. You do not want it on the inside walls of your smoker.

Start burning wood in kettle grill or similar container, then transfer glowing coals to firebox

5. Start your fire. While the meat is warming up to room temp, start making coals with your good smoking wood (see chart on page 92).

If you're using a big ol' smoker with an offset fire-box, I'd recommend against using charcoal briquettes. I think you get a better, truer, smoke flavor if you only use wood. It's a bit more expensive, but you're not barbecuing to save money in any case. You're barbecuing because it puts you in touch with your inner Kansas Citian. So, go all the way and just use wood.

In a kettle grill, a starter chimney, or an old wheelbarrow, start a fire with a few logs of wood. Don't use lighter fluid. Not ever. You don't want petrochemicals soaking into the wood. It'll ruin your fire, your smoke, and your meat. Use newspaper or a natural starter stick made of beeswax and wood chips to start the fire.

After the outsides of the logs have all burned black, some white ash is beginning to appear, and the flames have settled down a bit, use some big tongs to transfer these coals into the smoker.

Bring the temperature of the smoker up to about 250 degrees.

Here's a tip: buy way more wood than you think you'll need. Barbecue uses lots of it. If you have some left over, use it next time. It'll keep.

★ ★ ★ ★ ★ ★ ★ ★ ★ ★

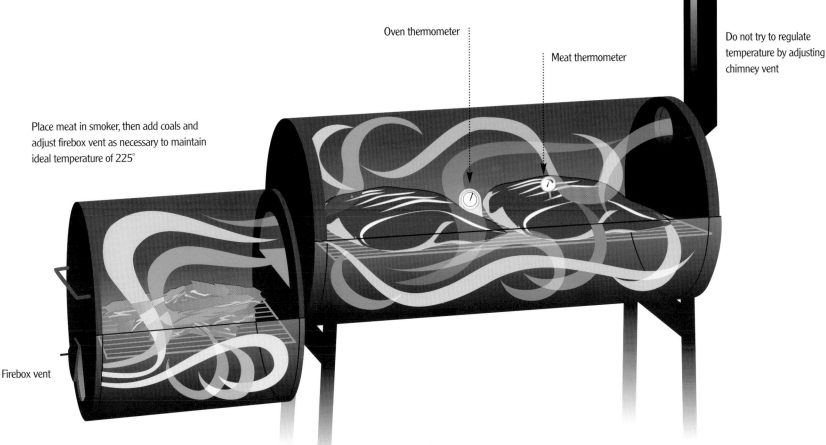

Oven thermometer

Meat thermometer

Do not try to regulate
temperature by adjusting
chimney vent

Place meat in smoker, then add coals and
adjust firebox vent as necessary to maintain
ideal temperature of 225°

Firebox vent

6. Put the meat in the smoker. You'll lose some heat when you open the door/lid, but that's okay. Just add some more coals.

Your main job for the next several hours is maintaining a temperature of about 225 degrees. This is tricky, but not impossible and actually it's a big part of the fun.

You'll need three thermometers for this operation: an instant-read meat thermometer to check the temperature of the meat near the end of the cooking process; an oven thermometer that will sit next to the meat on the grill (this will give you a quick temp check whenever you open the door/lid to mop or spritz the meat); and a big dial-style thermometer in the door/lid of the smoker. Not all smokers come equipped with a thermometer, but they almost all come with a hole in the door/lid where you can put one. Your local hardware or home improvement center will have thermometers that screw right into this hole.

7. Adjust the temp by adding a few more coals, tweaking the bottom vents in the firebox, or lifting the firebox lid an inch or two for a count of five. But do not, I repeat, do not try to adjust the temperature by adjusting the vent on the chimney. Leave this vent full open at all times. This allows the smoke to flow freely over the meat and out of the smoker. If this vent is closed even a little bit, the fire won't draw correctly, bad smoke will build up and the fire will die.

The temp will vary during the cooking. Don't sweat it. Your aim is to maintain an average temperature of about 225 degrees. Close the bottom firebox vents a bit when it gets too high and add coals when it gets too low.

During the cooking, try to minimize the number of times you open the smoking chamber door/lid. Each time you open the door/lid you let out a lot of heat, which prolongs the cooking time. You should open the door/lid only when you need to mop or spritz the meat. This principle also applies to lifting the firebox lid. You should only open the firebox when you need to add more coals to the fire.

8. Mop or spritz the meat every 45 minutes or so. I think spritzing is preferable to mopping because it's quicker and more efficient. This is important because the longer the door/lid is open the more heat you lose.

Get yourself a spray bottle at the hardware store, then consider all the lovely liquids that can be used in a barbecue spritz. These include apple juice, flavored vinegars, onion juice, garlic juice, (these last two are available in the spice section of most grocery stores), maple syrup, and infused cooking oils. Experiment. Come up with your own recipe. Keep in mind, however, that sugar, salt, herbs and spices will tend to clog up your spritzer.

Another thing to remember is that most alcohol is flammable. And there's fire inside that there pit. So don't use whiskey or other such in your spritz. It's dangerous. Drink your whiskey, don't spray it.

Spritz meat with liquid of your choice, every 45 minutes or so

9. The meat is (finally) done when the instant-read meat thermometer registers the appropriate reading for the type of meat you're cooking. Remove the meat from the smoker and let it rest on a platter for about 10-15 minutes before you start carving.

When you cut into the meat you'll notice that there's a nice pink ring around the edge. That's good. It's from all that tasty smoke. The pink is how you know it's barbecue. It doesn't mean the meat's not done. When you think about it, meat couldn't be done on the inside and raw on the outside, now could it?

Refer to meat thermometer to be sure meat is desired temperature

10. Carve the meat against the grain. This is especially important with brisket. The meat will be much tenderer.

If you've prepared a pork butt, you may want your friends and family to join you in "pickin'" it off the bone. This is an integral part of the barbecue ritual in the Carolinas, but in Kansas City pork is usually just chopped up.

If you don't regularly have your carving/butcher knives professionally sharpened, you should. Especially before a barbecue. You'll be pleased with the results.

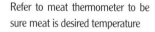

Let meat rest for 10-15 before serving. Carve against the grain.

★ ★ ★ ★ ★ ★ ★ ★ ★ ★

SMOKING IN A
KETTLE GRILL

In order to cook your meat to perfection, the proper setup of the grill is of the utmost importance. Here is a step-by-step look at what you need to do in order to ensure a delicious result.

1. Arrange approximately 20-25 charcoal briquettes on one side of the grill. Space the briquettes evenly in order to distribute the heat. Do not use "quick light" briquettes; they contain chemicals that may affect the flavor of your meat.

Place a drip pan filled with water, apple juice or beer on the other side of the grill. This will help keep the meat moist during the cooking process. Add more liquid as needed.

Soaking wood chips

Drip pan

2. Light the charcoal. Do not use lighter fluid. To produce a flavorful wood smoke, add chips of quality hardwoods to the fire, such as oak or hickory, that have been pre-soaked in water for 30 minutes.

3. Place meat on the grill rack opposite the charcoal and directly over the drip pan. Position the vent holes on the lid so as to draw the smoke over the meat. Use the lower-vent holes to control the temperature of the fire. Spritz the meat each time you lift the lid. The meat is done when the meat thermometer reads the appropriate temp for the specific kind of meat you're cooking.

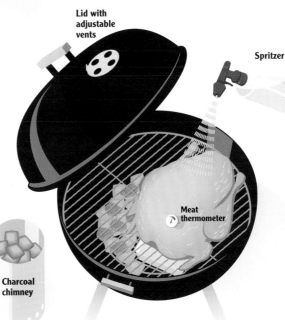

Lid with adjustable vents

Spritzer

Meat thermometer

Charcoal chimney

★ ★ ★ ★ ★ ★ ★ ★ ★ ★

RECIPES

There is no recipe for barbecue. Barbecue is a technique, not a recipe. But there are recipes for seasonings, sauces, and the good things you eat with barbecue.

SEASONINGS

Chef Paul Kirk has graciously provided us with three basic recipes for barbecue rubs. However, he agreed to do so only after I promised to include his standard caveat: *Don't rub your rubs*. In other words, just sprinkle the rub on the meat. Don't actually rub it in.

Here's another thing: feel free to add and subtract ingredients to suit your own taste and to customize these recipes. It's hard to mess up. As I've said, half the fun in barbecuing is the experimenting.

PAUL KIRK'S ALL-PURPOSE BARBECUE SEASONING

1 cup cane sugar
1/2 cup onion salt
1/2 cup Lawry's seasoned salt

2 tablespoons garlic salt
2 tablespoons celery salt
1/2 cup Hungarian Paprika
1/4 cup (Williams) chili powder
3 tablespoons fine grind black pepper
1 tablespoon lemon pepper
2 teaspoons dry mustard
1 teaspoon ground allspice
1 teaspoon ground ginger
1/2 teaspoon granulated garlic
1/2 teaspoon ground celery seed
1/2 teaspoon cayenne

Combine the sugar, onion, seasoned, garlic, celery salts, paprika, chili powder, pepper, lemon pepper, mustard, allspice, ginger, garlic, celery, and cayenne in a large bowl and blend well. Store in an airtight container, in a cool dark place.

PAUL KIRK'S BEEF BARBECUE RUB

1/4 cup cane sugar
2 tablespoons Hungarian paprika
2 tablespoons seasoned salt
2 tablespoons onion salt
2 tablespoons sea salt
1 tablespoon chili powder
1 tablespoon black pepper
1 tablespoon lemon pepper
1-tablespoon beef base powder
1 tablespoon white pepper
1 tablespoon dried rosemary, crushed
1 tablespoon cayenne
2 teaspoons ground thyme

Combine the sugar, paprika, seasoned salt, onion salt, sea salt, chili powder, black pepper, lemon pepper, beef base, white pepper, rosemary, cayenne and thyme, in a bowl and blend well. Sift and mix well. Store in a cool dark place.

PAUL KIRK'S BARBECUE PORK RUB

1/2 pound light brown sugar, dried*
2 tablespoons Hungarian paprika
1 tablespoon dry mustard
1 tablespoon onion salt
1 tablespoon celery salt
1 tablespoon chili seasoning
1 tablespoon seasoned salt
1 tablespoon black pepper

Combine ingredients in a bowl and blend well. Sift and blend well. Store in an airtight container in a cool dark place.

Yields about 1 1/2 cups.

*To dry brown sugar, place on a sheet pan and let sit for 2 to 3 hours; stir every hour. Sift out lumps.

SAUCES

In her 1824 landmark cookbook *The Virginia Housewife*, Mary Randolph describes an early American barbecue sauce made of red wine, "mushroom catsup," garlic, salt and pepper. *Hmmmm*. Not bad. But not nearly as tasty as these sauce recipes, supplied by our good friend Ardie Davis (the alter ego of sauce master supreme, Remus Powers). Davis has written his own book, *The Great BBQ Sauce Book*, (Ten Speed Press, 1999) which is the definitive guide to barbecue sauces.

A note from Remus himself precedes each of the recipes.

REMUS' AFRICAN GROUNDNUT BBQ SAUCE

We have enjoyed Groundnut Stew prepared by a friend from Sierra Leone. That's what inspired this sauce recipe. Here 'tis:

2 tablespoons canola or vegetable oil
1 medium onion, finely chopped
1 tablespoon mashed smoke-roasted garlic, or 4 cloves garlic, minced, if short on time
1 tablespoon red pepper flakes, or to taste
5 cups canned tomato sauce
1 cup orange juice
1 cup distilled vinegar
1 cup crunchy or smooth peanut butter (Remus prefers Jif)
1/2 cup cooked mashed sweet potato
2 tablespoons tamarind pulp or lime juice

In a large saucepan, heat oil over medium heat. Add onion, garlic and red pepper flakes, and saute until onion is tender. Add remaining ingredients. Bring to a boil. Reduce heat to medium low, and simmer for 5 to 10 minutes, stirring with a wooden spoon. Serve warm.

Refrigerate unused sauce up to one week.

Uses: As a table sauce with smoked or grilled chicken breast, pork ribs or beef brisket.

Remus originally contributed this recipe to *The Ultimate Barbecue Sauce Book*, by Jim Auchmutey and Susan Puckett, Atlanta, Ga.: Longstreet Press Inc., 1995 - pp. 64 & 65. Recipe used with permission.

REMUS POWERS' POSSUM TROT BBQ SAUCE

Possum Trot pioneers would no more think of putting tomato sauce on the barbecue than they'd think of putting Hollandaise sauce on their fried catfish. Pioneer barbecue, if seasoned at all, was more likely sprinkled with seasoned apple cider vinegar. Here's a basic recipe:

2 cups apple cider vinegar
2 tablespoons real Worcestershire Sauce (if caramel coloring is an ingredient, it isn't real)
1 teaspoon ground black pepper
Dash of ground cayenne or West African hot pepper (go easy; you can add more later if you want more fire)
1 teaspoon sea salt
1/4 cup prairie bee honey
1/4 cup molasses

Combine all ingredients in a stainless steel sauce pan. Heat, but don't boil. Stir with a wooden spoon until ingredients are blended. Let cool.

Store in glass cider vinegar jar. Will keep for weeks in your saddle bag or prairie schooner commissary chest.

★ ★ ★ ★ ★ ★ ★ ★ ★ ★

REMUS POWERS' KC URBAN PRAIRIE BBQ SAUCE

Tomato-based barbecue sauce arrived in Kansas City around the turn of the century, with urbanization, stockyards, an abundance of hickory and oak, and a flow of immigrants from Texas, Kentucky, Tennessee and other barbecue-friendly states.

Today's most popular KC sauces in restaurants and on market shelves range from sweet to tangy, mild to fiery. Sweet and mild holds the majority. One constant is a tomato base.

The following recipe is a mix of both sweet and tangy, with the accent on sweet. Pit drippings, an essential ingredient in some local greasehouse sauces, is optional, and not included in this recipe. Some cooks substitute a dab of butter with a dash of liquid smoke for pit drip flavor. Go easy. A little bit of liquid smoke goes a long way.

1 24-ounce bottle Heinz Tomato Ketchup
1 15-ounce can tomato sauce
1/3 cup apple cider vinegar
1 cup Brer Rabbit Molasses
1/2 cup packed brown sugar
1 teaspoon onion powder
1 teaspoon garlic powder
1/4 teaspoon celery seeds
1/4 teaspoon ground cumin
1/4 teaspoon ground cloves
1 teaspoon Louisiana hot pepper sauce or North Carolina Texas Pete hot pepper sauce

Put all ingredients in a stainless steel sauce pan and stir with a wooden spoon. Bring to a boil, reduce to simmer, and cook for 30 minutes, stirring occasionally.

Let cool. Pour into glass canning jars for storage.

WARNING!

Generally speaking, sauce should only be applied to barbecue after it's been cooked. Most Kansas City-style barbecue sauces have a relatively high sugar content. Sugar burns easily, which means that if you apply it to your barbecue while it's cooking it will encase your meat in sticky, black carbon.

★ ★ ★ ★ ★ ★ ★ ★ ★ ★
SAUSAGE

Lots of accomplished amateur cooks get the heebie-jeebies when it comes to making their own sausage. No need. If you've made meatloaf, you've made sausage. Here are some easy recipes for homemade sausage.

These sausages may be fried in a skillet as patties or boiled in water or beer as links, but frankly we've included these recipes in the book because sausage is so good cooked in your smoker along with your ribs, brisket and butt. They don't take as long to cook as your ribs, brisket and butt. About four hours at about 225 degrees should do it. Use your meat thermometer to check for doneness if you've got any questions.

PAUL KIRK'S
ITALIAN SAUSAGE

2 pounds pork butt, coarsely ground (have your butcher do it)
1 pound ground beef, coarsely ground
2 teaspoons granulated garlic
1 teaspoon Lawry's seasoned salt
1 teaspoon fennel seeds
1 teaspoon Italian seasoning
1/2 teaspoon crushed red pepper, optional or to taste
1/2 teaspoon fine grind black pepper
1/4 cup grated Romano cheese, optional
1/4 cup beef or chicken stock (dry wine, white or red, optional)

Combine the pork butt and beef in a large bowl; set aside. In a small bowl combine the garlic, salt, fennel seeds, Italian seasoning, red pepper and black pepper and blend well. Set aside.

Add 1/3 of the seasoning mixture and blend; repeat adding the seasoning a third at a time. Blend until it is all incorporated. Blend in the cheese if you are using it. Add the liquid if the meat is dry and needs some moisture; if the meat is moist enough omit it. Make into patties, loaves or sticks, or stuff into casings.

Makes about 3 pounds.

CHICKEN AND APPLE
SAUSAGE

1 cup apple cider
3 pounds boneless chicken-thigh meat, with skin, coarsely ground
2 1/4 ounces dried apples, diced
1 1/2 teaspoons sea salt
2 teaspoons rubbed sage
1/2 teaspoon white pepper
1/2 teaspoon ground allspice
1/2 teaspoon ground ginger
1/4 teaspoon ground cinnamon
1/8 teaspoon ground nutmeg
1 chicken bouillon cube dissolved in 2 tablespoons boiling water, cooled

In a non-reactive saucepan reduce the apple cider to 1/4 cup, until it's almost like apple syrup.

Cool and reserve. Combine the salt, sage, pepper, allspice, ginger, cinnamon and nutmeg in a small bowl and mix well. Combine the ground chicken, apples and chicken bouillon in a large bowl and blend well. Add the seasoning 1/3 at a time, kneading as you add the seasoning. Knead the mixture until it is sticky and binds together. Mold into patties, loaves, sticks or stuff into casings.

Makes about 3 pounds.

AUTHOR'S HOMEMADE SAUSAGE

4 pounds ground pork
1 pound thick sliced bacon
3 tablespoons salt
1 tablespoon black pepper
1 teaspoon cayenne pepper
1 tablespoon ground sage
1/8 teaspoon nutmeg
1 cup fresh flat leaf parsley, well packed
6 cloves fresh garlic, chopped fine
1 bottle Boulevard Unfiltered Wheat Beer
sausage casings

While bacon is still cold and unseparated, chop into small pieces. Combine ground pork, bacon, parsley and garlic and grind in meat grinder or process in food processor until thoroughly mixed. In small bowl combine the salt, pepper, nutmeg and sage and blend well.

Add 1/3 of the seasoning mixture to the meat mixture and blend thoroughly with hands; repeat adding the seasoning a third at a time. Add beer as needed if the mix needs moisture; if the meat is moist enough omit it. Make into patties, loaves or sticks, or stuff into casings.

★ ★ ★ ★ ★ ★ ★ ★ ★ ★

SIDE DISHES

We Kansas Citians have strong opinions about which are the best barbecue restaurants, the best barbecue sauces and the best barbecue events in town. However, we either really don't care all that much or we haven't made up our minds about which side dish goes best with barbecue.

This isn't the case in some of the nation's other barbecue regions, where specific side dishes are considered an integral part of the whole culinary, cultural experience that is barbecue.

In Kentucky, for example, barbecue is accompanied by a stewlike dish called burgoo, which is often made with mutton. Kentuckians must be very brave to eat burgoo, because a popular variation of the dish features squirrel brains, which, when eaten, are frequently fatal.

In the Carolinas, barbecue is served with a side of Brunswick Stew, a tomato-based soup made with chicken and pork shoulder. Another popular side dish sometimes served with Carolina barbecue is liver hash on rice. (*Eeeewwww!*)

In his book *Smokestack Lightning* (Farrar, Straus and Giroux, 1996), author Lolis Eric Elie features a recipe for grilled cabbage that calls for cramming cored cabbage heads with gobs of cream cheese, butter, garlic and Parmesan or Romano cheese, wrapping 'em in foil and cooking 'em on the grill. This flavorful, fragrant and fattening accompaniment would get my vote for Official Kansas City Barbecue Side Dish. (A modified version of this recipe is provided below.)

It's a shame that here in the Barbecue Capital of The World french fries are the default side dish served with most restaurant barbecue. What's that all about? French fries are not a unique regional cultural culinary experience. Not even in France. French fries go with franchised fast food, not lovingly slow-cooked barbecue.

Aside from fries, there seems to be an informal consensus that Kansas City barbecue is best accompanied by either baked beans, coleslaw or potato salad. This threesome appears on the grease-stained menus and lighted menu boards of virtually every barbecue joint in the metropolitan area.

When you think about it, potato salad, coleslaw and baked beans are a fairly accurate reflection of the collective Kansas City personality: mild-flavored, bordering on bland, slightly sweet with just a little tang. Safe and satisfying.

SWEET POTATO FRIES

If you insist on fries with your barbecue, at least make 'em sweet potato fries. They're easy to make and delicious.

Peel as many sweet potatoes as you need to satisfy yourself, your family or your guests, then cut them into french fry-sized strips, about 1/4 inch square. Pour enough peanut oil in a skillet to cover a batch of the fries. Heat the oil to around 350 degrees. Fry the potatoes until tender and golden brown. Sprinkle with salt. Better yet, sprinkle 'em with a liberal amount of your favorite barbecue rub.

Q HEADS

2 heads cabbage, cut in half and cored
3 (8 oz.) packages cream cheese, softened
1 cup finely chopped green onions
2 tablespoons fresh garlic, minced
2 sticks butter, softened
Salt and pepper

In a large bowl combine the cream cheese, butter, green onions, garlic, salt and pepper. Fill each cored half-cabbage head with cream cheese mixture. Really shove it in there between the leaves, so that when the cabbage cooks the cheese will melt and coat the cabbage well. Wrap each half head with heavy aluminum foil and cook in your smoker along with your barbecue. Cook until the cheese is completely melted and the cabbage is nice and tender. The outside of the heads may blacken during cooking. This is not a problem. Just peel 'em off before serving. Each half head may be cut into three sections for serving.

AUTHOR'S BARBECUE BEANS

1 pound dry navy beans
Canned chicken broth to cook the beans in
1 can tomato paste
1 (more or less) bottle of your favorite Kansas City-style barbecue sauce
1/2 cup (more or less) pure maple syrup
1 large yellow onion, chopped fine
1 pound bacon, chopped

Pick through the beans to check for stones. Rinse beans, cover in cold water and soak overnight. I usually stir into the water a couple tablespoons each of garlic powder and onion powder and a few bay leaves. After soaking, rinse beans thoroughly in a colander. Cover in chicken broth and cook until tender, not mushy. Drain. Chop uncooked bacon into 1/2-inch pieces. (This is best done when the bacon is still cold and unseparated.) Cook the bacon and chopped onion together until crispy and brown. Combine the beans, the bacon and onions (it's OK to

include some of the drippings), the tomato paste, the maple syrup and the barbecue sauce in a casserole. Here you can add or subtract wet ingredients according to taste and texture preference. Bake at 325 degrees for a week. Just kidding. Two or three hours should be fine. If you like a nice dark crust on top and a thicker consistency, bake the beans longer. If you like 'em a bit looser, don't bake 'em as long.

Here's an option for the hard-core barbecuer. When they're mixed and ready to bake, instead of cooking your beans in the oven, cook 'em in your smoker while you're making your barbecue. Put your beans on the rack under your brisket or butt or ribs and let all the meat drippings drip right into 'em while all that good wood smoke works its magic. If you're going to make your beans this way, you'll probably want to put them in a cast-iron pot or skillet for cooking, because the smoker might ruin a casserole dish.

AUTHOR'S POTATO SALAD

3 pounds new red potatoes, washed, boiled until fork tender
1 1/2 pounds fresh green beans, washed, snipped and blanched
1 small red onion, chopped fine
1 red bell pepper, chopped coarsely
1 yellow bell pepper, chopped coarsely
2 cloves fresh garlic, minced
2 to 3 tablespoons coarse Dijon mustard
Salt and freshly ground pepper to taste
One large bottle Paul Newman's original olive oil and vinegar salad dressing

Most potato salads served in barbecue joints are creamy concoctions made mostly of mushy white potatoes and a mayonnaise/mustard dressing. If you like that kind, you probably have a recipe from your mother or grandmother you can use to make some. This recipe's different. It's bright, colorful and crunchy. The best part is the fresh green beans. Toss all the ingredients together in a large bowl until the vegetables are well coated. This salad tastes best at room temperature, however. Because the oil and vinegar dressing tends to separate as it gets warmer, you'll need to toss it again just before serving.

AUTHOR'S COLESLAW

3 cups shredded green cabbage
3 cups shredded red cabbage
1 cup shredded carrot
1 small red onion, chopped fine
2 Granny Smith apples, peeled and cored, cut in matchstick-sized pieces
1 cup mayonnaise
2 tablespoons sugar
1 1/2 teaspoons cider vinegar
Salt and fresh ground pepper to taste
(For a little extra kick and color include 1/2 teaspoon cayenne pepper)

Combine ingredients in a large bowl and toss until cabbage, carrots, apples and onions are thoroughly coated. Cover and chill. May be served on top of a pulled or chopped barbecue pork sandwich.

★ ★ ★ ★ ★ ★ ★ ★ ★ ★

DESSERTS

AUTHOR'S SWEET POTATO PIE

I'll be honest with you, the very idea of making pie crust gives me the willies. I'll stay up all night long fussin' with the vents on my smoker, makin' coals, checking temps and spritzing my butt, supremely confident the whole time that the resulting barbecue will be a crowd pleaser, but attempting homemade pie crust scares me to death. *The Star's* food editor, Jill Wendholt Silva, calls this psychological phenomenon "fear of pieing."

My solution to this problem, like my solution to most problems, is avoidance. I use store-bought crusts. For that reason, this recipe does not include instructions for a pie crust. If you have a favorite homemade crust recipe, you can use it for this pie. You're braver than I.

Most recipes for sweet potato pie call for the same mix of spices typically used in a pumpkin pie. And what you end up with is a sweet potato pie that tastes like a pumpkin pie. What's the point in that? If you want a pumpkin pie, bake a pumpkin pie. This recipe is for a sweet potato pie and it uses only a little nutmeg. This allows the real flavor of the sweet potatoes to shine through.

1 9-inch pie shell, partially baked
2 pounds sweet potatoes (that's about 4-5 medium potatoes)
2 tablespoons unsalted butter, softened
3 large eggs, plus 3 yolks

1 cup sugar
1/2 teaspoon grated nutmeg
1/4 teaspoon salt
2-3 tablespoons bourbon or rye
1 tablespoon of maple syrup or molasses
1 teaspoon vanilla extract (Use the real stuff, folks. Not the artificially flavored junk.)
2/3 cup whole milk
1/4 cup brown sugar (for sprinkling on the bottom crust)

Some chefs say baking your sweet potatoes before mashing them produces a richer flavor than boiling. But I've tried it both ways and I can't really tell the difference. If you want to bake them, leave the skins on and put them in the oven at 350 degrees for about 45 minutes. Bake them just until they're tender to a fork. Don't overbake them. You don't want them to get too mushy.

If you decide to boil the potatoes instead of baking them, peel them first and boil them until

★ ★ ★ ★ ★ ★ ★ ★ ★ ★

they're tender. Again, don't overcook them.

While the sweet potatoes are still hot, mash them with a fork with the butter.

In a separate bowl, whisk together the eggs, egg yolks, sugar, nutmeg, salt, bourbon or rye, maple syrup or molasses, vanilla and milk. Gradually stir this mixture in with the mashed sweet potatoes.

Meanwhile, prepare your pie crust as you normally would for a pumpkin pie. Myself, I think partially baking the crust is important. It results in a less soggy crust. I put the unbaked pie shell in a pie pan, then place another pie pan, the same size, on top and press down slightly. I bake this for about 8 minutes, reduce heat to 325, remove the top pan and bake for another few minutes until the crust is a light golden brown.

Remove your partially baked crust from the oven and let it cool a bit. Then sprinkle the crust with the brown sugar and spoon in the sweet potato filling. (A variation is to spread a thin layer of peanut butter on the crust before filling. Use "natural"-style peanut butter, the kind without sugar or sweeteners.)

Bake the pie until the filling is set around the edges but still jiggles ever so slightly in the middle, about 45 minutes. I find I have to cover the edges of the crust with foil to prevent them from burning.

Serve with a scoop of vanilla ice cream or fresh whipped cream.

PECAN PIE

1 9-inch pie shell, partially baked *
1/3 cup melted butter
1/4 cup dark brown sugar, packed
1/2 cup corn syrup
1/2 cup pure cane syrup (or molasses)
4 large eggs, slightly beaten
2 teaspoons pure vanilla
1/3 cup heavy cream
1 1/2 to 2 cups whole pecans
Preheat oven to 450 degrees.
*To pre-bake pie shell see instructions for Author's Sweet Potato Pie above.

In a medium mixing bowl, blend melted butter with brown sugar, corn syrup, cane syrup or molasses, eggs, vanilla and cream. Stir together thoroughly. Fold in pecans. Pour into partially baked pie shell, turning over pecan halves right side up.

Place pie pan on a cookie sheet. Bake on bottom rack of oven until just set, around 35 to 45 minutes.

Cool completely before serving. Slice with a serrated knife.

CARAMEL BOURBON ICE CREAM SAUCE

1 cup sugar
3/4 cup heavy cream
3 tablespoons straight bourbon
1 teaspoon fresh lemon juice

In a heavy saucepan cook the sugar over medium low heat, stirring constantly with a whisk, until melted and lightly caramel colored. Cook, without stirring, swirling pan, until deep golden. Remove pan from heat. Slowly and carefully stir in cream, bourbon and lemon juice. Caramel will start to harden during this process.

Return pan to heat and simmer, until the caramel is dissolved. Serve on vanilla ice cream.

PEACH COBBLER

1 cup sugar
3 tablespoons cornstarch
1/2 teaspoon cinnamon
1/4 teaspoon nutmeg
3 (15 oz.) cans canned peaches
2 tablespoons butter
1 cup flour
2 tablespoons sugar
1 1/2 teaspoons baking powder
1/2 teaspoon salt
1/3 cup butter
1 egg, plus one egg yolk
1/4 cup milk
2 teaspoons pure vanilla extract
1 tablespoon sugar

Preheat oven to 375 degrees.

Combine one cup sugar, cornstarch, cinnamon and nutmeg in large bowl. Add peach slices and toss to coat. Grease 8-inch square pan with butter and add peaches. In a medium bowl, whisk together the flour, 2 tablespoons sugar, baking powder and salt. Cut in the 1/3 cup butter until coarse crumbs are formed. In a small bowl beat the eggs and yolk. Add the milk and vanilla and mix well. Combine milk mixture with flour mixture until flour is just moistened. Don't overmix. Drop batter by large spoonfuls onto the peaches. Sprinkle 1 tablespoon sugar over the batter. Bake for 25-30 minutes or until cobbler is golden brown.

CHAPTER FIVE

BARBECUE NATION

Barbecue, as we've defined it, is a uniquely American food tradition. But not all parts of America share in this tradition. As we pointed out earlier, barbecue is concentrated primarily in the American South. And though Kansas City is considered a Midwestern town, it has historical and cultural links to the South. The states of North Carolina and Texas have strong barbecue traditions, as do the cities of Owensboro, Kentucky, and Memphis. None of these places, however, is the Barbecue Capital of the World.

NORTH CAROLINA

North Carolina would be the only other part of the country with a legitimate claim to the title Barbecue Capital of the World, except that everyone knows that capitals are *cities*, not whole states.

A couple of years back, when I was editor of *Star Magazine*, I invited Kathleen Purvis, food critic for *The Charlotte Observer*, to write about Carolina barbecue for our annual barbecue edition. She graciously agreed and produced one of my all-time favorite pieces of barbecue writing. Here it is.

— D.W.

Allow me to present my credentials: Southern-bred and Georgia-born, I have spent more than half of my 41 years as a Carolina Tar Heel.

All that is a polite way of saying: Bubba, I know from barbecue.

When it comes to introductions in my part of the world, your barbecue credentials are as critical as your politics, your religion and your choice of college basketball teams. Jesse Helms doesn't engender as much controversy as the debate over whether to put tomato in your sauce.

Now it's true that some of my Carolina brethren (and sister-en) harbor a bit of porcine prejudice. Pork, they will insist, is the only true barbecue. But I was raised by open-minded people who liked to travel. So I can be nonpartisan and say that a good Texas brisket is a fine thing, and the only truly bad rib is a burned one.

Your barbecue only has to be pork if you want it to actually be great.

There. See how open-minded I can be?

In my decade or so of covering food for *The Charlotte Observer*, I have been called on countless times to serve as a barbecue guide. Call me an ambassador of the pits.

I have sat up through the night with a whole pig in a smoker. I have judged at least eight barbecue competitions, and I have guided many an amateur through the intricacies of their first pig picking.

(It's a social thing; I'll explain later.)

Thanks to our network of interstates, our sunny economy and our business climate, the Carolinas are regularly invaded — oops, sorry, wrong century — visited by people from other regions. And before they put down their bags and grab the real-estate ads, they are on the phone to me, in search of the barbecue grail. So let me explain a few things:

Barbecue is a noun, not a verb. If you really want to make Carolinians grit our teeth, invite us over for dinner, then say, "We're barbecuing. How do you like your hamburger?" That thing with hot coals is a grill or a pit, not a barbecue. And what you put over your coals is barbecue only if it is pork. Not hot dogs.

We talk sweet, but we eat vinegar. There are three basic Carolinas sauce belts: In eastern North Carolina, around Raleigh, and some areas of South Carolina, sauce is simply vinegar and red pepper. In western Carolina, from Lexington to the mountains, sauce is vinegar, red pepper and a little tomato, usually ketchup. And in a few pockets of South Carolina, mostly around Columbia, sauce is yellow and has mustard.

Some people think eastern Carolina's vinegar sauce goes back to an ancient distrust of tomatoes. I tend to think it's more a residue of our Colonial past, when

people liked food tart. It's really only important if you need something to chat about while you wait for your chopped plate.

We can go whole hog. Or we can be butt-heads. I'm not being rude: That's the easiest way to explain the other big division in our barbecue. In eastern N.C., they cook the whole pig, then chop the meat with a little sauce mixed in. In western N.C., around Lexington, they use the Boston butt, which is the fatty part of the shoulder. They still chop it but not as fine. Some menus offer barbecue chopped or sliced, but I think sliced is just a polite way of saying, "You aren't from around here, are you?"

Cook it low and slow. The trick to making something great out of cheap, fatty cuts of pork is to cook it slowly, so the fat melts out and the meat is falling-apart tender.

Smoky flavor is important, but don't go overboard — it shouldn't taste like you're sucking on a stick. While gas cookers have made inroads all around the state, wood coal, burned down from hickory, is still the best. It's hot, it's messy, it puts off smoke. And it makes the very best 'cue.

True barbecue season isn't summer, it's fall. In the old days, that's when people butchered hogs. And because that is also close to election season, barbecue and politics have always been bedfellows in the Carolinas. If you get invited to a political barbecue, or even a friendly backyard one, you may encounter something called a "pig picking."

A pig picking is a whole pig, cooked slow all night. You stand over the pig on the grill and pull off what you want,

called picking. Then you fill your plate with cole slaw and hush puppies and grab a slice of white bread. The bread isn't for a sandwich (the sign of the amateur). Pig pickings usually involve small plastic forks. So use the bread to push meat onto your fork, then use it at the end to mop up the last drippings from your plate.

It also makes a handy thing to gesture with. Because once you have a pig picking under your belt, your barbecue credentials are established. And you are free to move on to other important matters.

Who do you like for the ACC championship this year?

— Kathleen Purvis
The Charlotte Observer

In researching Owensboro barbecue I came across a connection that I believe merits further investigation. There appears to be an association between sheep and whiskey.

Consider Scotland. The place is practically covered in sheep. The only thing they have more of in Scotland than sheep is whisky. (Astute readers will notice here that in Scotland whiskey is spelled "whisky," without the "e.")

My theory is that sheep are the reason the Scots became so good at making scotch whisky. There are so many sheep in Scotland it was inevitable that at some point the Scots would begin eating the sheep. That's when they developed haggis.

That's right. **Haggis**.

Haggis — which is no doubt named for the retching sound people make when they eat it — is made by stuffing a sheep's stomach bag with sheep suet, and chopped up sheep's lungs, liver, bladder and heart, plus some oatmeal and onion. This revolting concoction is then boiled for four or five hours. You need lots of whisky after eating haggis to help you forget you ate it.

Now let's consider America's own national spirit: bourbon. Where was bourbon born and raised? Kentucky, where instead of haggisizing they barbecue them.

It seems that regions of the world that excel in sheep production sooner or later perfect the art of whiskey making. Now would probably be a good time to invest in distilleries in New Zealand.

— D.W.

★ ★ ★ ★ ★ ★ ★ ★ ★

KENTUCKY

Believe it or not, the town of Owensboro, Kentucky, actually thinks it's the barbecue capital of the world.

Isn't that just laughable?

What makes it even funnier is that what Owensboronians specialize in is barbecue *mutton*.

That's right. Barbecued sheep.

Every year it seems the 60,000 or so citizens of Owensboro literally set their streets on fire during its annual barbecue festival. Apparently they construct barbecue pits right on the city streets and start cookin' them sheep.

Now, I have to tell you I like that image: Takin' it to the streets. There's something radical about giving over the municipal roadways to barbecue. We should try that here.

As we mentioned early on, Owensboro has another claim to barbecue fame. A Mr. Harry Green might very well have been America's first barbecue restaurateur. He is said to have opened a joint there in 1890.

MEMPHIS

Memphis is another one of the places that considers itself to be the Barbecue Capital of The World.

It isn't.

But Memphis gave us Henry Perry. And Memphis gave us Carolyn Wells. And for those two gifts Kansas City should be forever grateful.

Reluctantly, we are forced to acknowledge that there are in Memphis at least as many barbecue joints per capita as there are in Kansas City. And the city is home to one of the country's oldest and certainly the rowdiest barbecue competition, the Memphis in May World Championship Barbecue Cooking Contest, which was founded in 1978.

But Memphis' claim to barbecue supremacy is limited by its insistence that barbecue is pork and pork only. It may be pork shoulder — pulled or chopped — ribs or whole hog, but it's got to be pork in Memphis.

In Kansas City we have a far more inclusive view of barbecue. As Carolyn Wells, who, as we indicated, is a one-time Memphian who has since converted to Kansas Cityism, is known to say "In Kansas City, if it moves we barbecue it."

In Memphis the choice is not pork or beef, it's *wet or dry*. I'm told folks in Memphis get quite worked up about this issue, which has apparently divided the city into two opposing camps. Basically it comes down to the question "Do you like your ribs with sauce or without?" to which Kansas Citians answer "Yes."

TEXAS

Beverly Bundy is a graduate of the University of Missouri-Columbia, home of the best school of journalism in the U.S. of A. Plus she's one of the best food critics in America. Given that she's a superbly trained and gifted journalist, sworn to accuracy and fairness, and that she's a culinary expert of the highest order, and that she actually lived not all that far from Kansas City, well, you'd think that she'd know better than to assert that Texas barbecue is best. Here's what she had to say on the subject in *Star Magazine's* 2000 barbecue edition.

— D.W.

In Texas, barbecue is a religion. Like pilgrims on a hadj, the sons and daughters of the Alamo risk parched asphalt miles and rampaging javelina in search of the holiest smoke. Church revivals, family reunions and campaign fund-raisers are all excuses for digging pits or loading up portable smokers where celebrants can genuflect.

Except for some California-bound vegans marooned in Midland-Odessa while their van is repaired, everyone in Texas is a believer.

The cathedrals vary, from the sanctified grounds of the New Zion Missionary Baptist Church Barbecue in Huntsville to the school desk and car hood seating of the hallowed Sonny Bryan's Smokehouse in Dallas. But one tenet runs through Texas barbecue dogma - the chosen worship at the altar of the cow.

It was the emigrant German butchers of the Texas Hill Country around Austin who delivered us to this Valhallah. Looking for a use for the brisket, a cut so tough a sidewinder would think twice about a bite, these wily men began smoking it to goodness in the back of their shops.

Brisket is ubiquitous to Texas barbecue — coated with a dry spice rub and then smoked for hours, with a tomato-based sauce served on the side. Ordered either sliced or chopped, it is the standard by which any 'cue is judged. The sliced meat should have a rosy ring just under the surface, a tell-tale sign of trial by fire.

The German butchers left another legacy in central Texas. The wurst of their native forests became a link between two cultures. Elgin, so-declared by the wise minds of the Texas Legislature, is the sausage capital of

the state. It was at the Southside Market & BBQ there that Elgin Hot Guts were born. Originally, the links were all-beef sausages christened with a hellacious amount of red pepper. But now some of the fire is gone and legions of imitators are making sausage with boutique ingredients like pork and turkey.

Texans will accept pork in their barbecue, as long as it is in rib form - the skin crusty from caramelization, the pink moist flesh rouged with that rosy ring. Other than that, they want no ifs, ands or butts.

After a century of barbecue, there have been some changes. Kreuz Market in Lockhart, the Lourdes of Texas barbecue, has become a house divided by a family feud. Now Kreuz is Smitty's and Kreuz has built a new location. But at both restaurants, meat is ordered by the pound and the counterman whacks off a portion from a sleeve of saltines for the carbohydrate portion of the meal.

Only recently have Texas barbecue joints added chicken to the canon. Possibly in response to so many Yankees trailing U-Hauls, or possibly because there seems no way to muzzle those folks at the American Heart Association, smoked bird is now widely available. But you won't see many native Texans ordering it. And if they do, they have the sense to get it to go.

— Beverly Bundy
The Fort Worth Star-Telegram

MICHIGAN

Some places have no barbecue. Generally speaking, Michigan is one of those places. You can find some reasonably good barbecue in Detroit. But in the part of Michigan I came from there's not only no barbecue, there are no food traditions at all.

Until moving here, I had lived all my adult life in Kalamazoo, Michigan. Kalamazoo has no

real food traditions of its own. The political and economic influence of Dutch immigrants in Kalamazoo is pervasive, but their culinary influence is minimal. The only Dutch food I can recall is a deadly, doughy, dumplinglike dish called fatballs. Kalamazooans have so far declined to adopt fatballs as their city's signature food.

Cities without a food of their own are vulnerable to poorly formed civic identities because, after all, you are what you eat.

Kansas City eats barbecue. It's our food. And it says something about us.

Consider the specifics of barbecue for a moment. First of all, barbecue is cooked very slowly over low heat. "Slow and low" is the motto of Kansas City's pitmasters.

Second, barbecue is cooked indirectly by a wood fire and it's flavored by the fire's smoke. Sometimes it's marinated — again, slowly — so the flavors have plenty of time to soak in. Barbecue is crusty on the outside, but tender on the inside. Barbecue has a complex flavor — smoky, savory, sweet and spicy. Kansas City barbecue sauce doesn't assault your mouth with flame-hot heat. Rather the heat builds slowly to a nice warm glow.

Most important, barbecue is a substantial food. It's not fancy, but it is satisfying.

Like barbecue, Kansas Citians can't be rushed. We don't make snap decisions. We like to let things soak in before we act. We are tenderhearted. We can be sweet. But there is a complexity to our character that is frequently underestimated. Beneath the surface there is a fire, though it sometimes takes time for our passions to surface. We're not real fancy, but we are a people of substance.

If you are what you eat, I'd rather live in the City of Barbecue than the City of Fatballs.

★ ★ ★ ★ ★

...AND BACK AGAIN

In Michigan, all turkeys taste the same. It's not that they don't taste good. They do. Thanksgiving dinner is as happily anticipated in Michigan as it is anywhere. There's just not much imagination or variation in the way turkeys are cooked up there. Stuff it and stick it in the oven.

Above right: Michigan has nice bridges, but no barbecue. The Mackinac Bridge, shown here, is five miles long and connects Michigan's Upper and Lower Peninsulas.

That's about it.

Not so here in Kansas City. In Kansas City, Thanksgiving turkeys are prepared in a variety of wonderful ways.

Like jazz, the increasingly popular practice of deep-frying turkeys seems to have migrated to Kansas City from New Orleans. Jazz, however, is an acquired taste. Deep-fried turkeys are not. They're the juiciest, tenderest birds you'll ever eat. You can buy turkey fryers for about 80 bucks. Buy one and try it. You'll be giving your Thanksgiving guests a treat for which they'll be truly grateful. (Be warned. Deep-frying a turkey is strictly an outdoor activity. Keep the young 'uns safely inside and far away from the hot oil.)

Another Kansas City tradition is to arrange for your turkey to be smoked at a smokehouse or local barbecue joint. Lil' Jake's at 13th and Grand excels at this. So does Fritz's Superior Meat Co. on State Line near 103rd.

Finally, because this is Kansas City, after all, a lot of us barbecue our Thanksgiving turkeys in our backyards.

Last Thanksgiving a heathery veil of fragrant smoke hung in the trees of our neighborhood. It was a sublimely Kansas City scene: men lovingly tending their barbecue. As morning receded to midday, some of us drifted out toward the street, beer or whiskey in hand, where we met to exchange grilling and smoking knowledge.

When you think about it, barbecuing is an authentic Thanksgiving practice. The first Thanksgiving was, after all, a community affair, not unlike a neighborhood block party, a church potluck or a big ol' barbecue. Families didn't hole up in their houses. They came together to express their gratitude for their collective blessings.

We Kansas Citians should be grateful to be here. Here where our traditions reflect a colorful civic personality and a rich diversity of regional and ethnic influences.

Three Thanksgivings ago, my parents were here visiting for the holiday. They live in Michigan. They were too polite to say so out loud, but both of them were clearly concerned about the turkey slowly smoking in my Weber out in the driveway.

More than once my mom told me to take my time and not to rush. She wanted to be sure the turkey was cooked through.

"We're in no hurry," she said.

And when I would go outside to put more wood chunks on the fire or mop the turkey with my secret baste, my dad would follow me to look over my shoulder and say things like, "Well, I'll be" and "Would you look at that."

Hours later when we were eating, my father couldn't stop raving about the food. "Where'd you learn to cook like this?" he asked.

"It's part of the entrance exam you have to take before you can move to Kansas City," I said. "They won't let you in unless you can demonstrate basic barbecuing aptitude."

After dinner, my dad and I stood out in the driveway drinking coffee. We watched as my next-door neighbor, Terry, carefully removed his turkey from his grill.

"This Kansas City is quite a place," said my father.

AFTERWORD

★ ★ ★ ★ ★ ★ ★ ★ ★

Henry Perry paid me a visit last night.

As it had for weeks, my alarm clock woke me at 2:30 a.m. whereupon I cursed to myself, got out of bed, pulled on jeans and a sweat shirt and went downstairs to write the last few pages of this book.

And there he was. Sitting at my kitchen table drinking a glass of my best whiskey. He wore a freshly pressed black suit, with a starched white shirt and dark blue necktie. A black porkpie hat sat next to him on the table.

"I do believe this is rye," he said, holding the glass up to the light, admiring the red gold liquid.

"Yes, sir. It is," I said.

"Spirits for the spirit," he smiled. And he took a slow sip.

"Do you know who I am?" he asked.

"You appear to be Henry Perry," I said as I sat down. "At least you look like the pictures I've seen of Henry Perry. Of course, you've been dead for 60 years, so I'm either hallucinating, or I'm dead, too."

"You're not hallucinating," he said. "And neither of us is dead. I just don't live *here* anymore."

"This book has finally gotten the best of me," I mumbled.

"That's why I come to see you," he said. "You've been takin' this whole barbecue thing a little too seriously."

"I'm surprised to hear that coming from you. From what I've read, I'd say you took barbecue pretty seriously."

"Barbecue was my *business,* young man. And I took my business seriously."

"So barbecue was just a business to you, nothing more?"

Mr. Perry frowned.

"A business isn't nothing."

"That's not what I meant…"

He interrupted me.

"Why have you got yourself so worked up about barbecue?"

"Because it's important. It's a unique expression of our cultural identity."

He frowned more deeply.

"Son, barbecue is just a way to cook meat. That's *all* it is. A way to cook meat."

"How can you say that?" I exclaimed.

He sighed.

"You need a little perspective, boy. Here. Put this on," he said, handing me his hat.

I placed it on my head.

★ ★ ★ ★ ★

And just like that, Henry Perry and I were standing in a dark, dank little room with a low ceiling and a greasy concrete floor.

My fingers were still holding the brim of the porkpie.

"Where are we?" I asked.

"This is Jones Bar-B-Que," replied Perry. "And that there is their pit."

He motioned in the direction of a big, blackened brick box with a huge cast-iron door.

"I know this place," I said. "It's on 10th Street in KCK."

"The very one," he said. "Gentleman by the name of Hezekiah built this place just about the time I passed on. Big fella. Almost 7 foot tall. Size 13 shoes."

I nodded.

"Grace Harris once told a reporter that she used to come here on Saturday nights for pigs' feet and snouts."

"They was popular back then," said Perry. "These days most folks can afford better meat, so they don't buy feets and snouts much anymore."

"What are we doin' here?" I asked. "Is this some kind of *A Christmas Carol* or 'It's a Wonderful Life' deal?"

"You could say that. Like I said, you need some perspective. Look, here comes Deborah Jones. Don't worry. She can't see us."

"Just like in the movies," I murmured.

Deborah Jones was carrying an armload of logs. She stepped down into a recessed area on the other side of the brick pit and dropped the wood on the floor. She stepped back out, took off her coat and walked gingerly over to a desk and chair, where she hung her coat on the back of the chair. She leaned on the edge of the desk.

★ ★ ★ ★ ★ ★ ★ ★ ★ ★

"She looks tired," I said. "And it looks like her leg is hurt."

"It's her foot," said Perry. "Bad circulation. And she is tired. It's 4:30 in the morning and she just finished her shift at the post office where she's a mail handler. She is tired. Yet here she is. Gettin' the fire goin' for the barbecue."

Deborah Jones was shoving logs into an opening at the bottom of the pit.

"Why?" I asked. "I mean, she's got a decent job..."

"Because it's her business," Perry said. "She and her sister, Mary, inherited this business from their father, Leavy Jones Sr., who worked for Hezekiah himself. It's their business now. And they're tryin' to make a better life for themselves."

Deborah had taken some briskets out of a refrigerator and was placing them in the pit.

Perry continued.

"The other morning Mary was in here early repairing the pit. And she *was* tired, too. Because when she's not here, she's workin' another job as a nurse. But she never complains. Not ever. In fact, there's hardly anybody who smiles as much as Mary Jones. She lives her life with an attitude of gratitude. That's somethin' these women got from their father. He told 'em, 'You don't make a negative out of a positive. You find a way to make a positive out of a negative.' That's the spirit livin' in these Jones sisters.

"Leavy Jones and his wife were married for 54 years. They had eight children. He never made it past second grade, but he became a fine electrician. And then he worked here, too, at this place, for ol' Hezekiah, to help make ends meet.

"Eventually he taught the business to Deborah.

She and Mary have been keepin' it goin' since."

Deborah was operating a meat grinder. We watched her work.

"She's making sausage," said Perry. "Her father's secret recipe. It's their best-selling item."

"Seems like a hard life," I said.

"I can tell you this," he replied. "Right about now she's not thinkin' about expressing her cultural identity."

★ ★ ★ ★ ★

"Well, son," he said. "Tip your hat to the lady."

I touched the brim of the porkpie hat and suddenly Henry Perry and I were sitting in lawn chairs on the grassy bank of a park pond. The sun was high in the sky. Mr. Perry had taken off his suit coat and rolled up his shirtsleeves.

"Man!" he exclaimed. "I forgot how hot it gets here."

We were surrounded by hundreds of little makeshift campsites where teams of men and women were cooking barbecue in massive black smokers under brightly colored awnings.

"I know where we are," I said. "This is the Lenexa Barbeque Battle. It gets this hot here every year."

A fragrant blue haze hung over the place. Children raced from site to site, shouting and laughing. A Delbert McClinton record was playing over a loudspeaker. An official-looking trio of women with name badges and clipboards zipped by on a golf cart.

"Hey," I said. "There goes Carolyn Wells. I wish I could introduce you. She'd be thrilled to meet you."

"Sounds like you know what's goin' on here

pretty well," he said. "Why don't you tell me about it while we stroll around a bit."

We got up and started a slow walk around the park.

"This is one of the biggest and best barbecue contests there is. It's the Kansas state championship. People come from all over the country to compete here."

"Why exactly do you think that is?"

"Well, just look at these people. They *love* barbecue. Barbecue is like a *religion* to them."

About then we came upon a pristine black mega-smoker mounted on a shiny red trailer. Under a banner proclaiming that this was the "Bum Steers" barbecue team, four or five middle-aged men and a woman laughed and teased as they arranged slices of brisket on beds of leafy lettuce in Styrofoam containers. The man in charge had a trim white beard and an intense smile. As he and his pals labored over their barbecue, he offered them encouragement and beer. From a nearby boom box, Bruce Springsteen was making a point about proving it all night.

"Son, I'm lookin' at the same people you are and all I see is folks having fun. Religion is about salvation. And it can be a joyful thing. But barbecue has never *saved* anybody. These people aren't here to *worship*. They're here to cook and eat and enjoy one another's company. This isn't *church*. It's just a barbecue."

I was embarrassed.

"It seems like more than that."

Perry nodded his head toward the team leader.

"That's Jim Powers there. He and his wife, Cindy, have been competing in these contests for almost 10 years. They go to 10 or 12 of 'em every year. Jim puts a lot of time and money into it. And he wants to win. He likes being the best at what he does. But if you asked him how he got started with all this barbecuing, the first thing he'd tell you is he likes to feed people. Simple as that. It satisfies him."

I considered the possibility that everything I had thought to be true about barbecue was wrong, while Henry Perry admired Jim Powers' big black smoker.

"Lord, if that ain't a beauty," he said, shaking his head. "What I couldn't have done with a cooker like that when I was here."

★ ★ ★ ★ ★

"All right, boy," he said. "Time to move along."

I knew what to do. I touched the hat.

We were back at my house, only not in the kitchen. We were outside in my driveway, where my smoker was all fired up, cooking some barbecue. The sun was just coming up.

"Smells good, son," said Henry Perry. "Smells like you know what you're doin'."

I was about to thank him for his compliment when I heard my back door open, then close. I turned and saw *myself* coming out of the house with a cup of coffee in hand.

"This is *too* weird," I said.

"I know what you mean," said Perry. "It takes some getting used to."

I watched myself check the temp on the smoker, then go over and sit on the little retaining wall by the hedgeapple trees where I sipped my coffee.

"You look happy," Perry observed.

"It's one of the things I enjoy most," I replied.

"Preserving Kansas City's cultural identity must be very satisfying."

"OK. I get your point. When I'm out here cooking I'm not thinking about anything but the barbecue and gettin' it done right, because in about six hours my in-laws are all gonna be here ready to eat."

I looked at Henry Perry.

"But I do worry," I said. "Everywhere around the world local traditions are being threatened by global corporations wanting to make money by making everything the same. I worry that some big fast-food company is going to come to Kansas City and start selling some abomination they call 'barbecue' and they're going to sell it cheap and soon everybody is going to forget what real barbecue is and that'll be the end of that. A glorious tradition gone. Our local identity lost."

The very thought of it upset me deeply. I scowled.

Perry considered my argument for a moment.

"So, does your family like your barbecue?"

"Actually they do."

"Why? Because it's an expression of their cultural identity?"

"They like it because it tastes good."

"Ah. Because it tastes good."

We watched as I got up from my seat on the wall and went over to tend the fire.

"Son, when I was here, jazz was the music everybody liked. It was in all the clubs. Kansas City was famous for it. Back then you could remember a jazz tune and sing a jazz tune because it actually *had* a tune. But when jazz stopped bein' music everyday people could sing or whistle around the house, well, then it stopped

bein' popular..."

I interrupted.

"When jazz didn't *taste* good anymore, people stopped *eating* it."

"Exactly. If your wife's family didn't *like* your barbecue they wouldn't eat it. And as long as the Jones sisters and Jim Powers and all the others are makin' barbecue that tastes good, Kansas City's 'cultural identity' is safe. Relax, son. Barbecue is in good hands."

The other me opened the smoker and applied apple juice with a spray bottle to the ribs and brisket inside.

"Yessir," Perry said. "That sure does smell good."

He put his hand on my shoulder.

"Let's go back in the house."

★ ★ ★ ★ ★

In the kitchen I poured myself a glass of the rye and we sat at the table and drank in silence. Upstairs somebody got out of bed, and Henry Perry stood up.

"I guess I'll be needin' my hat," he said.

I took the porkpie from my head and handed it to him.

"Thank you, Mr. Perry."

"My pleasure. Good luck with your book."

The old man took one last sip of whiskey.

"You wanna take the bottle?" I asked.

He put his hat on.

"No thank you. The whiskey is a lot better where I'm goin'."

Then, just before he left, he turned to me and smiled.

"But the barbecue is better here." ★

★ ★ ★ ★ ★ ★ ★ ★ ★ ★

Above: Mary and Deborah Jones in their wood pit at Jones Bar-B-Q in Kansas City, Kansas

APPENDICES

The barbecue joints listed here are the primary reason why Kansas City is the Barbecue Capital of the World. With almost 100 great barbecue restaurants in the greater metro area you could eat at a different one each weekend for almost two years. By then, no doubt, a few new establishments would have opened and, alas, a few existing places would have closed. The following listing is, to the best of our knowledge, complete as of April, 2001.

Arthur Bryant's Barbecue
(two locations)
1727 Brooklyn
Kansas City MO 64127
(816) 231-1123

8201 NE Birmingham
Kansas City MO 64161
(Ameristar Casino)
(816) 414-7474

Amazin' Grace's Barbeque
(The Grand Emporium)
3832 Main
Kansas City MO 64111
(816) 531-1504

Backdraft Barbecue
1016 NW Woods Chapel Rd.
Blue Springs MO 64015
(816) 224-4227

BB's Lawnside Bar-B.Q.
1205 East 85th
Kansas City MO 64131
(816) 822-7427

Bates City Bar-B-Que
(two locations)
2nd and Market
Bates City MO 64011
(816) 625-4961

6493 Quivira
Shawnee KS 66216
(913) 962-7447

Big Q
2117 S. 34th St.
Kansas City KS 66106
(913) 362-6980

Big T's Bar-B—Q
9409 Blue Ridge
Kansas City MO 64138
(816) 767-0905

Boardroom Bar B-Q
9600 Antioch
Overland Park KS 66212
(913) 642-6273

Carl's Fish and Ribs
8116 NE 69 Hwy
Pleasant Valley MO 64068
(816) 453-2626

Dave's Sweet Savour Bar BQ
5440 Blue Ridge Cut Off
Kansas City MO 64133
(816) 737-3252

The Filling Station
333 S.E. Douglas
Lee's Summit MO 64063
(816) 347-0794

Fiorella's Jack Stack Barbecue
(three locations)
9520 Metcalf
Overland Park KS 66212
(913) 385-7427

101 W. 22nd
Kansas City MO 64108
(816) 472-7427

13441 Holmes
Kansas City MO 64145
(816) 942-9141

Gates Bar-B-Q
(six locations)
Main office: (816) 923-0900
3201 Main
Kansas City MO 64110
(816) 753-0828

1221 Brooklyn
Kansas City MO 64127
(816) 483-3880

103rd and State Line
Leawood KS 66206
(913) 383-1752

10th and State Avenue
Kansas City KS 66101
(913) 621-1134

E. Emanuel Cleaver II
Kansas City MO 64110
(816) 531-7522

10440 E. 40 Hwy
Independence MO 64055
(816) 353-5880

Greenwood Barbecue
205 E. Main St
Greenwood MO 64034
(816) 537-5577

Hickory Log Bar-B-Q
5047 Wellbom Lane
Kansas City KS 66104
(913) 287-9560

Summit Hickory Pit
1012 S.E. Blue Parkway
Lee's Summit MO 64063
(816) 246-4434

Hayward's Pit Bar-B-Que
11051 Antioch
Overland Park KS 66210
(913) 451-8080

Lil' Jake's Eat and Beat It
1227 Grand
Kansas City MO 64106
(816) 283-0880

Jake Edward's
5107 Main
Kansas City MO 64112
(816) 531-8878

Johnny's Hickory House
5959 Broadmoor
Mission KS 66202
(913) 432-0777

Jones Bar-B-Q
1805 N. 10th
Kansas City KS 66104
(913) 281-4148

★ ★ ★ ★ ★ ★ ★ ★ ★

K.C. Masterpiece
(two locations)
4747 Wyandotte
Kansas City MO 64112
(816) 531-3332

10985 Metcalf
Shawnee Mission KS 66210
(913) 345-1199

Knight's B-B-Q
6225 Winner Road
Kansas City MO 64125
(816) 483-7610

L.C.'s Barbeque
(two locations)
5800 Blue Parkway
Kansas City MO 64129
(816) 923-4484

95th St. and I-35
Lenexa KS 66215
(913) 894-4500

Laura's & Emmie's Bar-B-Q 'N Stuff
7445 Prospect
Kansas City MO 64132
(816) 361-1890

Marty's BBQ
2516 N.E. Vivion
Kansas City MO 64118
(816) 453-2222

Nichols Bar-B-Que & Grill
110 Cunningham Parkway
Kansas City MO 64102
(816) 331-4363

135th St. Bar-B-Que
325 E. 135th
Kansas City MO 64145
(816) 941-4296

Oden's BBQ & Steak-more
1302 N. Scott
Belton MO 64102
(816) 322-3072

Oklahoma Joe's Barbeque
3002 W. 47th
Kansas City KS 66103
(913) 722-3366

Papa Lew's Barbecue
1504 Prospect Ave.
Kansas City MO 64127
(816) 231-2800

Parker's Barbecue
10925 NW 45 Hwy
Parkville MO 64152
(816) 746-1300

Pioneer Trails Barbecue
121 W. Lexington
Independence MO 64050
(816) 254-2466

Earl Quick's Bar-B-Q
1007 Merriam Lane
Kansas City KS 66103
(913) 236-7228

Quick's Seventh Street Bar-B-Que
709 Cheyenne
Kansas City KS 66105
(913) 371-1599

Rawhide BBQ
101 North 169 Highway
Smithville MO 64089
(816) 532-9588

R&B B.B.Q
4900 N.E. Vivion
Kansas City MO 64119
(816) 452-5058

R&J Barbeque
8401 Parallel Parkway
Kansas City KS 66112
(913) 299-1311

Ribs-N Stuff
(two locations)
802 West U.S. 40
Blue Springs MO 64015
(816) 224-2833

240 N.W. Oldham Parkway
Lee's Summit MO 64081
(816) 525-7427

Rosedale Barbeque
600 Southwest Blvd
Kansas City KS 66103
(913) 262-0343

Santa Fe Trail Bar-B-Q
2049 E. Santa Fe
Olathe KS 66062
(913) 782-7352

Say Barbeque
967 W. Liberty Dr.
Liberty MO 64068
(816) 781-7427

Smokin' Joe's Bar-B-Q
(two locations)
101 Southwest Blvd
Kansas City MO 64108
(816) 421-2282

519 E. Santa Fe
Olathe KS 66061
(913) 780-5511

Smokin' Roy's B-B-Q
125 S. Lake St.
Pleasant Hill MO 64080
(816) 540-6395

Southern Nook Bar BQ
416 E. Mill St.
Liberty MO 64068
(816) 407-1408

Smoke-Me-Baby Bar-B-Que
10328 Blue Ridge Blvd.
Kansas City MO 64134
(816) 763-8787

Smokebox BBQ Cafe
10020 N. Executive Hills Blvd.
Kansas City MO 64153
(816) 891-8011

Smoke Stack Bar-B-Q
8129 Hickman Mills Drive
Kansas City MO 64132
(816) 333-2011

Smoke Stack BBQ
8920 Wornall
Kansas City MO 64114
(816) 444-5542

Smoke Stack Barbecue
8250 N. Church Rd.
Kansas City, MO 64158
(816) 781-7822

Smokehouse Bar-B-Que
(three locations)
19000 E. 39th St.
Independence MO 64057
(816) 795-5555

6304 N. Oak Trafficway
Gladstone MO 64118

(816) 454-4500
11900 Shawnee Mission Pkwy
Shawnee KS 66216
(913) 631-1888

Snead's Bar-B-Q
171st and Hwy 58
Belton MO 64012
(816) 331-9858

Stilwell Smokehouse
19300 Metcalf
Stilwell KS 66085
(913) 897-1110

Three Friends Bar-B-Q
2461 Prospect
Kansas City MO 64127
(816) 231-9753

We B Smokin'
32580 Airport Drive
Paola KS 66071
(913) 755-0175

William's Bar B-Q
7510 E. 87th
Kansas City MO 64138
(816) 313-7771

Winslow's City Market Barbecue
20 E. 5th St.
Kansas City MO 64106
(816) 471-7427

Wyandot B-B-Q (two locations)
8441 State Ave.
Wyandot KS 66112
(913) 788-7554

7215 W. 75th
Overland Park KS 66204
(913) 341-0609

Zap Bar-B-Q
5550 Troost
Kansas City MO 64110
(816) 444-1119

Zarda Bar-B-Q
(three locations)
11931 W. 87th St.
Lenexa KS 66215
(913) 492-2330

214 N. 7 Hwy
Blue Springs MO 64014
(816) 229-9999

7121 W. 135th
Overland Park KS 66223
(913) 681-1118 (scheduled to Oct. of 2001)

Bob's Pit Bar-B-Que
1902 W. Wall St.
Harrisonville MO 64701
(816) 380-3882

Biffle's Smoke House Bar-B-Q
103 NE 2nd St.
Concordia MO 64020
(660) 463-7232

Buffalo Bob's Smokehouse
719 Massachusetts
Lawrence KS 66044
(785) 841-6400

Cattleman's BBQ
2 W. Amity
Louisburg KS 66053
913 837-5361

Coss' Smokehouse
612 E. Main St.
Gardner KS 66030
(913) 856-7053

Daniel's Bar-B-Q
215 West St.
Tonganoxie KS 66086
(913) 369-2440

Longhorn Barbecue
228 Oak
Bonner Springs KS 66012
(913) 441-0494

Outlaw's Barbecue
129 E. Washington St.
Kearney MO 64060
(816) 628-6500

Pat's Blue Rib'n BarBeQue
1618 W. 23rd
Lawrence KS 66046
(785) 865-1618

Quick's Bar-B-Q
1527 W. 6th St.
Lawrence KS 66044
(785) 841-3322

Ribs & More
13 W. 21st St.
Higginsville MO 64037
(660) 584-5400

The Santa Fe Depot Diner
781 Shawnee
Leavenworth KS 66048
(913) 651-6336

T-N-T BBQ
304 North 7 Hwy
Pleasant Hill MO 64080
(816) 540-6008

Wabash BBQ
646 S Kansas Ave.
Excelsior Springs, Missouri
816-630-7700

Branding Iron Barbeque
2027 N. Commercial
Harrisonville MO 64701
(816) 380-2214

Smokin' Steer
500 S. Commercial
Harrisonville MO 64701
(816) 380 7800

Above: Cindy and Jim Powers and the big ol' smoker they use to win barbecue championships as part of the Bum Steers barbecue team.

★ ★ ★ ★ ★ ★ ★ ★ ★

MISSOURI AND KANSAS
BARBECUE CONTESTS

Missouri and Kansas host over 30 barbecue contests each year. Here is a listing of some of these competitions. Contact the Kansas City Barbeque Society at (816) 765-5891 for dates and specific information for each contest, or the local chambers of commerce.

APRIL

Rotary Rock 'n Ribs BBQ Festival
Springfield, Missouri

**Annual Marshall
Rotary Club Cookoff**
Marshall, Missouri

MAY

Annual Red Hot & Wild
Topeka, Kansas

Sertoma's Annual Cook-off
Lawrence, Kansas

Harry's Smoke Out
Grandview, Missouri

Blues & BBQ
Sedalia, Missouri

**Annual Blue Devil Cookoff
Sunflower State BBQ Championship**
Bonner Springs, Kansas

**Katy Town Festival
Barbeque Contest**
Parsons, Kansas

JUNE

**Annual North Kansas City
Barbecue Contest**
North Kansas City, Missouri

**McClouth BBQ Blowout
Northeast Kansas State
BBQ Championship**
McClouth, Kansas

Tonganoxie Days BBQ
Tonganoxie, Kansas

**Annual Raytown State
Championship Barbecue**
Raytown, Missouri

**Annual Great Lenexa
Barbeque Battle
Kansas State Championship**
Lenexa, Kansas

Annual Platte City BBQ Fest
Platte City, Missouri

Black River BBQ
Poplar Bluff, Missouri

Old Town Barbecue Cookoff
Wichita, Kansas

JULY

Annual City of Osceola BBQ
Osceola, Missouri

**Annual Johnson County Fair
BBQ Contest**
Warrensburg, Missouri

**Annual Central Kansas State
Barbeque Cookoff**
Great Bend, Kansas

**Kansas Speedway/Oklahoma Joe's
BBQ Contest**
Kansas City, Kansas

**Annual Heartland Festival
and BBQ Cookoff**
Olathe, Kansas

Dodge City Days Barbeque
Dodge City, Kansas

AUGUST

**Annual Laurie Hillbilly
Bar-B-Q Cookoff**
Sunrise Beach, Missouri

**Flint Hills Beef Fest
Blues & BBQ**
Emporia, Kansas

Roots Fest BBQ Championship
Paola, Kansas

SEPTEMBER

Annual Cass County Cookoff
Harrisonville, Missouri

**Annual Leavenworth
Charity BBQ Cook-off**
Leavenworth, Kansas

**Annual Blue Springs
State Championship**
Barbeque Blaze-off

**Annual Jesse James
Barbeque Cookout**
Kearney, Missouri

**Annual Springfield Missouri
Sertoma Bar-B-Q Cookoff**
Springfield, Missouri

**Annual Shawnee Great Grillers
State Championship**
Shawnee, Kansas

OCTOBER

Annual American Royal Barbecue
Kansas City, Missouri

★ ★ ★ ★ ★ ★ ★ ★ ★

PHOTO CREDITS

Unless otherwise noted, all photographers credited are current or former employees of *The Kansas City Star.*
Photographs not credited here are from the files of *The Kansas City Star* library.

i.   John Sleezer

2.   Top left: Rich Sugg. Top right: Garvey Scott.
Bottom left: Ed Zurga, Special to The Star.
Bottom right: Stephen Pingry

15.   Middle and right: Courtesy of Western Historical Manuscripts
Collection, University of Missouri-Kansas City

17.   Courtesy of The Kansas City Call

18.   Courtesy of Bob Miller

21.   Courtesy of Gates and Son Bar-B-Q

22-23.   Courtesy of Pete Armato

26-27.   John Sleezer

28.   Top: Marcio Jose Sanchez

32.   Courtesy of the Gates family

34.   Talis Bergmanis

35.   Tim Janicke

37.   Tim Janicke

38.   Jim Barcus

39.   Julie Jacobson

41.   Tim Janicke

43.   Tim Janicke

44-45.   Tim Janicke

47.   Tim Janicke

48-49.   Jim Barcus

50.   Talis Bergmanis

51.   Julie Jacobson

52.   Joe Henderson

53.   Beverly Bynum

55.   Tim Janicke

56.   Jim Barcus

57.   Julie Jacobson

59.   John Sleezer

63.   Jim Barcus

64.   Talis Bergmanis

65.   Jim Barcus

66.   Tim Janicke

68.   Rich Sugg

69.   Tim Janicke

70.   Talis Bergmanis

71.   Left: Tim Janicke.
Right: Talis Bergmanis

73.   Tim Janicke

76.   Tim Janicke

77.   Top left: David Pulliam.
Top right: Talis Bergmanis.
Bottom left and right: Talis Bergmanis.
Center: Wendy Yang

78.   Shane Keyser

79.   Sean Galvin

80.   Sean Galvin

82.   Left: Marcio Jose Sanchez.
Right: Armando Solares

83.   Jennifer LaPolla

85.   Julie Jacobson

87.   Beverly Bynum

88.   Mike Ransdell

90.   Jim Barcus

92.   Jim Barcus

95.   Jim Barcus

98.   Top left and right: Talis Bergmanis.
Bottom right: Joe Ledford

104.   Tim Janicke

113.   Patrick Schneider

114.   Jim Barcus

115.   Paul Moseley

116-117.   KnightRidderTribune

118.   Comstock

122.   Julie Jacobson

125.   Jim Barcus